Clare and Zac - this book is dedicated to you.
The two most beautiful souls, my
unique, delightful children.
My little test pads... you got the best
of your mama and the worst!
But I always got the best of you. The strong, courageous,
insightful and inspirational young woman and young
man that you are now brings joy to my heart.
You make me happy. You make me proud.
You make me complete
Thank you for your love, acceptance and
forgiveness. I am truly blessed and I love the
both of you endlessly and eternally.

For Clare Suzanne
and
Zachary William Frederick
(Oh yes I did!!)
xxx

Sunshine 4 Your Soul

Positive, Powerful Parenting . . .
One Breath, One Step, One Day at a Time.

MARION INGERSON-HEART

BALBOA
PRESS
A DIVISION OF HAY HOUSE

Balboa Press books may be ordered through booksellers or by contacting:

Balboa Press
A Division of Hay House
1663 Liberty Drive
Bloomington, IN 47403
www.balboapress.co.uk
1 (877) 407-4847

Because of the dynamic nature of the Internet, any web addresses or
links contained in this book may have changed since publication and
may no longer be valid. The views expressed in this work are solely those
of the author and do not necessarily reflect the views of the publisher,
and the publisher hereby disclaims any responsibility for them.

The author of this book does not dispense medical advice or prescribe the use
of any technique as a form of treatment for physical, emotional, or medical
problems without the advice of a physician, either directly or indirectly. The
intent of the author is only to offer information of a general nature to help
you in your quest for emotional and spiritual well-being. In the event you use
any of the information in this book for yourself, which is your constitutional
right, the author and the publisher assume no responsibility for your actions.

Any people depicted in stock imagery provided by Getty Images are
models, and such images are being used for illustrative purposes only.
Certain stock imagery © Getty Images.

Print information available on the last page.

ISBN: 978-1-9822-8059-8 (sc)
ISBN: 978-1-9822-8060-4 (e)

Balboa Press rev. date: 05/01/2019

CONTENTS

INTRODUCTION

How lovely to meet you!

I'm so happy that you are reading this and thinking about taking some steps towards finding your personal power and creating greater balance and harmony in your life.

When you're feeling low, when you're feeling stuck, when you're feeling as if your strength, your energy, your power has all drained away... Well, I just want to let you know that those are feelings I understand really well!

I know how hard it can be to imagine that anything can change.

I know how hard it is to believe that things can improve when you don't feel as if you have any control over what might be going on in your life.

I know how easy it is to just keep doing the same thing over and over again because you don't know what else to do, whilst desperately hoping that something will change, a miracle will happen, and life will magically get better.

And I know how easy it can be to end up feeling a bit lost, a bit desperate and wondering what on earth you can do next.

I've been there with you, honestly I have!

But I also know that change *is* possible, and just the simple fact that you are now reading this speaks volumes. You chose to pick this book up for a reason, and I truly believe this could be the start of a wonderful journey for you. You've made a decision, you're on your way, and I'm delighted to walk beside you for a while.

So first of all I'm just going to ask you to bear with me while I tell you about me and my decision to finally write this book. I feel it's important for you to know what motivated me and why. I'm going to share some very personal experiences with you because I think it will not only provide you with an understanding of who I am, but more importantly, why I feel I may be able to guide you towards greater personal and family harmony.

Whilst I don't know your story and haven't walked in your shoes, I do believe that my own life experiences have provided me with opportunities for reflection and learning which has created an awareness that allowed me to make some good, positive changes. I'm so grateful to be able to say I've reached a point where my relationships seem more fulfilling and harmonious. And I feel calmer, more balanced, and more able to keep going!

And so if any of my experiences and what I've learned can offer support to you, then that makes me happy.

Of course, this hasn't happened overnight. And it's still a work in progress because that is what life is! Isn't it interesting that when you meet someone and ask how they are, they often say 'Oh, I'm getting there.' I used to say it myself. But then I started to think about it, and my question now is - where is 'there?!' What does 'there' look like? And do we ever actually get 'there?!'

So I now wonder if maybe it's more about the actual journey and not the destination. It's the things we experience along the way, the knowledge and understanding that we gain, the emotions we feel, the life we live just one breath, one step, one day at a time.

So basically, whatever I offer you in this book is based on my own personal learning curve and what I gained from it. I didn't spend years studying and I don't have any letters after my name. So you certainly won't find a lot of psychobabble or clever, highbrow explanations.

Hopefully what you will find is some sensible support and a useful tool here and there.

And an opportunity to look at things from a different perspective with someone who has maybe been where you are. Along with equal measures of honesty, understanding, openness, and some humour too!

I won't judge you, I won't criticise you, and you certainly won't hear me telling you what you 'should' do. I tend not to use the 'sh' word. I try not to tell other people what they should do, and I don't tell myself either!

The way I see it is this. People will give you advice, and of course they are generally well meaning and trying to be supportive and helpful, which is lovely. We all need advice and support at times.

However, I personally feel that we don't really need the word 'should' in our lives. It sounds a bit like an order to me, and when we are looking for help and support we don't need orders.

Let me give you a quick example of what I mean.

Your lovely, well meaning friend knows you have been feeling stressed and fed up lately, and is trying to find a way to help you.

'Oh,' she says, 'you should get up early every morning and go for a walk because it's so good for you'. Well yes, she is quite right, we all know that walking is good for us. It not only benefits us physically, but mentally and emotionally too. Endorphins and all those marvellous things are released and we can't help but feel a bit better after a good walk.

So there you are, she's given you a good piece of advice and you've been told, you **should** go for a walk every morning!

Now, this person, your friend, has taken the time to offer you this helpful advice. You value their friendship and it's lovely that she wants to help you. But now if you don't take her advice and start going for that early morning walk you could appear ungrateful, even a bit rude. And if you don't follow her advice you are potentially risking upsetting her because she's told you that you *should*!

Of course, we know On a conscious level that this isn't strictly true, but the message you have received prompts unconscious beliefs and if you are feeling low this won't really help.

So there you are, telling yourself you *should* take the walk, come on, get up, get going, do what you know is good for you.

But just maybe you are now feeling a little more pressure, and at this point any added pressure is just what you really don't need. You've been giving yourself a hard enough time anyway, and when we're feeling low we can often self sabotage and not do the things that we know might help us feel better.

So this might just be one more thing to feel bad about.

Now it may seem as if I am making a big deal out of one small word! But later on in this book I'm going to tell you more about how the words we hear and the messages we receive can affect us quite deeply.

So I much prefer using the word 'could'.

If you hear your friend saying, 'you *could* get up and go for a walk…'

You can say to yourself 'yes, I *could* try getting up every morning to go for a walk because I know it would be good for me'.

This is a gentler approach, creating more potential for the opportunity, the possibility, and maybe you are better able to make this decision without the pressure of the implied order.

I just believe we need to find ways to treat ourselves kindly, and the words we use are part of that.

Ok, enough of *should* and *could*, hopefully you now have a little flavour of what I am trying to say here. And as I mentioned, we will find out more later on.

When I started writing this eight years ago my initial focus was to offer support and advice to parents of teenagers and older children. And it still is very much geared for that.

However, over time it has evolved into a book that all parents could benefit from. And maybe not just parents. I'm sure I could have used it at different stages in my life as I had a pretty negative outlook and I sometimes felt a bit useless. And a bit bonkers. And obviously not good enough because everyone else seemed to be coping alright so why wasn't I?!

I honestly never realised that other people may have felt the same, I thought it was all just me.

And then when I became a parent, things became even more challenging in different ways. So I would have loved to read a book that reassured me and helped me to feel better about myself. A book that could support and guide me towards becoming more confident and powerful. A book that told me I was alright being who I was. In fact, I was more than alright - I was pretty unique, amazing and fabulous! Because I am - and so are you.

I'm convinced that parenting is probably the most difficult job in the whole wide world. But of course it's the one that provides us with life's greatest rewards. I guess it would be fair to sum it up by saying that it's the most incredible, wonderful, terrifying, life altering experience of all! I just hope that by reading my introduction, and then my book, you will find a little support, advice, and maybe a tool kit to reach into where you could pick out a little something to help you feel better and effect a positive change for you and yours.

But all without any orders, criticism, judgements, or 'shoulds!'

Well, that's almost it for now, but before we go any further I want to say this. The most important thing to remember is that it all starts with you.

Take care of yourself, be kind to yourself, and support yourself in a loving, positive way.

Think about how to let go of old habits that don't serve you well anymore.

Find out how to take small steps towards making some changes.

And please don't panic, I will show you how!

Fear can be our most difficult challenge can't it?

Fear, and the limiting beliefs we have about ourselves.

Fear of failure, fear of criticism, fear of judgement.

Fear of change... and then the fear of NOT changing!

But here's the thing.

Even though you know something isn't working and you feel that nothing seems to be changing.

Even though your life might seem to be going round in circles and you feel stuck in the hamster wheel of negativity

Even though the daily grind seems inevitably endless...

Please remember this

You ALWAYS have the power

Of course, it may not feel as if you have, but you do.

You just need to learn where it is and how to find it!

So why not try something different?

What have you got to lose?

Go on! Seize the moment, grab life by the scruff of the neck and give it a good shake... And then take a deep breath and read on!

MARION JILL WRIGHT - THAT'S ME!

I was born on 17th September 1959, after my poor mother laboured for four days to give birth. She had endured her pregnancy throughout one of the hottest summers on record and it must have seemed like an endless torture. By the time I arrived she was almost two weeks over her due date and I finally weighed in at 10lbs 10 oz. Oh yes, I made my presence felt... poor old mum Apparently visitors to the hospital used to go to the baby ward to see the huge baby that looked more like a three month old than a newborn.

Ah well, I always was a something of an attention seeker!

I'm one of three children, an oldest child with two beautiful sisters. And the irony of it all is that my mother never wanted any children at all!

I can recall feeling a bit put out when I learned that she had actually never wanted any children, not even one, and certainly not three! My mother's life was mapped out, and apparently when she met and married our father she told him quite clearly that children were not going to be an option. She was dedicated to her bell ringing, country dancing, guiding and brownies.

However, as these things can tend to happen, within a year she was pregnant.

Poor old mum, pregnancy was an unwelcome surprise and her life had to change in ways that she really hadn't expected, or wanted.

* * *

Before I carry on, I want to share a copy of the letter that my grandmother, Mary Ingerson (nee Leonard) sent to my mother a few weeks before she married my father in the spring of 1958. I was so delighted when my mother gave it to me as it's a very special keepsake.

> Feb 1958
>
> My Dear Bee,
>
> I felt I ought to write some words of advice, especially as I haven't been able to be with you during the last few weeks, but in reflection I feel I am not sure what to say. Marriage brings its problems to everyone in different ways and as the glamour wears off (yes it will, even for <u>you</u>) we have to set about adjusting ourselves to life for and with another,

someone <u>more important</u> than oneself. When this doesn't seem easy, try to remember that the other person is probably struggling too, and the solution is to pool the problems and try to solve them together. "Give and take" sounds old fashioned, but it is the answer - and the "give" has to come first, often having the appearance of being out of proportion, but the happiness of having given brings its own reward. So that is what I mean when I wish you long and deep happiness in your new life.

If it is ordained that you must have children, try to accept them as a challenge, you <u>could</u> make a lovely mother - and if you only have half the joy I have had through the love and devotion of my children you will be blessed.

Mother.

'If it is ordained that you must have children, try to accept them as a challenge...' So much in that sentence, and mum really had no choice other than to accept the challenge! But she did it with courage and strength, and in many ways she *was* a lovely mother.

* * *

3

My mother was an incredible woman. She was strong, kind, and very intelligent. If someone needed help she offered it in her usual sensible and practical manner. Growing up, she too was something of a rebel. Her father wanted her to join the Civil Service and follow in his footsteps, but mum had other ideas. She decided that she wanted to become a pig farmer, and enrolled on a course entitled 'Agriculture adapted for women' at Bicton farming college in Devon. She loved her time at Bicton, and she never did become a civil servant. Instead she spent quite a few years in her twenties working at various different farms around the country.

Mum loved everything about nature and was a real animal lover. As we grew up we learned the names of wildflowers, how to identify birds from their song, and spent many a happy hour collecting shells and feathers with her.

She rang the bells at St Martins church in Ruislip for fifty years and was a valued member of the bell ringing band.

Mum's great passion was for her Brownies and Guides, and she embraced her role as Brown Owl and then Guide Captain with great commitment and dedication.

When she died in 2014, many of her guides came to the funeral. I hadn't realised how many of them had kept in touch with her throughout the years, and the letters of condolence all followed a similar theme. Mother had been a wonderful role model to them, supportive, sensible, kind and they felt their lives had benefited from being led by her. It was lovely to hear all the positive comments and very comforting to hear how she had positively influenced so many young women.

One of the things Mum enjoyed the most was organising the summer camp. Camp fires, songs, she loved everything about it. I have some wonderful memories of those times and she first took me to camp with her when I was about 20 months. I love this photo, she looks so happy.

So, as I said, my mother was a good person, with many wonderful qualities. However, woe betide you if you irked her, she certainly didn't suffer fools gladly! She had no qualms about letting you know if you irritated her and to be honest I grew up feeling that I was never quite 'good enough' in her presence. I wanted to be hugged and cuddled and told I was wonderful - but that just wasn't what mum was all about. She showed her love for us in practical ways, as I imagine did many women of her generation. But I yearned for positive praise, sweet words, cuddles, and most of all her approval.

Mum wasn't particularly enlightened when it came to the 'emotional' stuff in life, and could probably best be described as something of a naive soul. She had lived such a lovely sheltered middle class life, was a 'decent' woman who didn't drink, smoke, or use bad language - and then she met my father! To be honest, it was an incredible mismatch, but she fell in love with big Bob Wright and that was that.

My dad was a working class man and had lived a very different kind of life. He told us that his father was run down and killed by a horse drawn milk float when he was a young child, and then his mother died of cancer when he was aged 13. He only ever showed us a handful of pictures of his family, and curiously I can't recall him showing us a photo of himself as a child at any age. No baby photos, nothing.

We never knew much about our fathers life, his childhood, or his family. And we only ever met his younger brother and his family a few times over the years.

In later years he would pour me a large rum and tell me stories about his life. Apparently known as 'Mad Bob Wright', he carried a gun and used it on more than one occasion. He quite happily told me how he shot a man in the leg when in his local pub one night because he had foolishly made a joke about my father wearing 'spats'. Yes, I know, quite why he was wearing spats is beyond me, maybe he was experiencing delusions of gangster!

There was also a grim story about a friend whose daughter was molested, and although the police caught the abuser, apparently the trial was mishandled and the perpetrator was found not guilty and released.

I remember sharing my father's understandable outrage at this travesty of justice as I listened to his ranting whilst watching the spittle building up in the corners of his mouth. But then he smiled, and leaning closer he whispered in my ear, 'Killed and buried with the same shovel, son... killed and buried with the same shovel.'

Did I believe him? Yes I did, I felt I had no reason to doubt him.

But who knows what was true and what wasn't. There weren't many people who could verify or deny his stories, and I wasn't going to question him. He was my father, and our parents don't tell lies!

My father could be very kind and generous, and it mattered to him that people thought well of him. He was intelligent and resourceful, and he had a strong work ethic. But he wasn't well educated man, and this clearly creating feelings of inadequacy. Unfortunately he was also an abusive man in more ways than one. Prone to violent outbursts of temper, he would suddenly explode, and his behaviour could become quite terrifying. He grew increasingly abusive throughout my childhood, and his rage and frustration was usually directed towards me. I can still clearly see his big, red, angry face as he shouted, roared and threatened to kill me, with his eyes glaring, teeth clenched, his huge hands balled into fists.

He chased me through the house for the first time when I was about 7 years old, and can I remember the panic and terror I felt as I ran, knowing he was right behind me. It felt as if the floor were shaking from his pounding feet. I tore through the lounge as fast as I could, heart pumping wildly as I waited for the moment when I would feel him grab me, catch me, kick me, hit me. I ran through the hallway and up the stairs, with no idea by now whether he was still behind me, I couldn't hear anything other than my panting breath. I dived into our tiny box room which was full of junk and suitcases and pressed myself into the corner behind the door, hoping and praying he wouldn't come in and find me. Luckily, he didn't. Either he had just given up, couldn't be bothered, or was satisfied that he had scared me enough, I don't really know which. So I stayed there for a while, and when I finally came out I went and hid my wet knickers in the washing basket, totally ashamed that I had wet myself.

Then there was the day we were all watching television as we sat round the dinner table eating our evening meal. I said something that upset him, and it was as if he had been poked with a cattle prod. With a roar of rage he picked up the dining table and hurled it up into the air, smashing everything on it. I ran across the room, not really knowing where I was going or what to do, only to then find myself pinned into a chair by the weight of the table which he had thrown across the room at me. I can't really remember what happened next, but I guess I just stayed there, unable to move until he left the room and my mum and sisters rescued me.

I do recall that the stains from the food and the teapot remained on the polystyrene ceiling tiles for years as a grim and constant reminder of his temper!

Really, he was a frightening man when in this state, but we all kind of accepted it and got on with it. What else was there to do? Mum did her best to calm him down when she could, but sometimes we would just find ourselves clearing up the mess of whatever he had thrown, broken, torn apart.

One day he lost his temper again and ripped the huge wooden office that stood in our front room apart with his bare hands. Mum quietly asked me to take the broken pieces down the garden to the bonfire heap and as I took another load I looked at my little sisters faces. They were sitting halfway up the stairs, huddled together, and hugging each other for comfort. I remember how my chest hurt and my stomach churned to see their little faces looking at me with fear and sadness.

I don't remember actually feeling frightened myself. I was just boiling with anger, furious and frustrated that I couldn't stop him and that once again we all had to put up with his rage and destructive behaviour.

I loved my sisters, and felt very protective of them.

But I also felt I failed them because I couldn't protect them from my father.

One thing I would never admit to myself - or anyone else - was that I was frightened of him. Oh dear me no, that would be weak and silly and foolish, and allowing him to win. I wasn't having that. So I concentrated on becoming strong and tough and not letting him see how much he scared and hurt me.

In a way, I guess I just dealt with it all by emulating him and the way he behaved. I worked hard at hiding my feelings behind a nice big wall of anger. Oh and believe me, I was angry! I used to tell my sisters that one day I would kill him. I convinced myself I hated him, and focused on that feeling. I couldn't control what he did, but I could control and hide my feelings, and I became very good at it! No tears, no weakness, just lots and lots of anger.

Although I felt very protective towards my sisters, I was also bossy big sister, often telling them what to do and trying to make them let me join in their games. At first I would ask nicely but if they said no I would try and force them, maybe push them around a bit. They shared a bedroom which was fine by me as I loved having a bedroom of my own. But at times I was keenly aware of the bond they shared and I guess that sometimes I felt a bit isolated and left out.

Lone wolf, that was me, always on my own and mostly I liked it that way.

So, looking back, I think it's fair to say that I didn't feel emotionally nurtured or particularly loved, although a lot of that could have been to do with my lone wolf attitude. As the years went by my fathers rages and violent behaviour increased, and I often had an unsettled feeling inside, never knowing what was coming next.

For many years I kind of believed that I was a 'difficult' child, and my parents found it hard to love me. I was sulky and prickly and I suppose I thought I didn't deserve love, and it was all my fault. Quite *what* was my fault I don't really know, but maybe I had done something to make myself unlovable.

I didn't have many friends at school which most of the time didn't really bother me. I fought with the boys, I was very strong and they knew it! And I looked down on the girls. I thought they were pathetic and weak and I didn't want to be associated with them. There were the occasional times when I felt rather alone and keenly aware that I wasn't popular so I would try to get along with the girls and be part of the 'in' crowd. But inevitably after a short while they just became annoying and silly and I fell out with them again!

So I carried on fighting with the boys, alienating myself from the girls, and told myself I didn't care.

School was alright, but often boring and I found the lessons tediously slow. However, my real passion was for the weekly drama lessons. Maybe I loved it because I could become something else, or someone else, for a while. I also loved the attention I received from acting a part in a play. I thrived on entertaining and making people laugh. I adored hearing that I was good at something. I wasn't at all self conscious, I threw my heart and soul into any part I played, and I revelled in the praise and compliments I received.

I was given all the 'character' parts, but I secretly yearned to be Cinderella, or Snow White, or Sleeping Beauty. I can remember feeling disappointed every year when I was once again awarded the part of the 'baddie' in the Christmas play. I was very tall, and by the age of eleven I was almost a head taller than most of them. And with my national health glasses and scowling face, I certainly wasn't ticking the boxes of the stereotypical pretty princess from the story books. In fact, a less suitable and appropriate candidate for the princess crown would have been hard to find! But still, every year I kept hoping I would be chosen to play the heroine instead of the ugly sister or wicked witch.

I guess I just wanted to feel beautiful, and I wanted to be loved.

When I was nine, the school decided that I needed to be moved up a year. I was very intelligent, and being a September baby I was older than all the others in my class. So I guess that the school thought it would be beneficial for me to be in a class with older children doing more advanced work.

Well, I went from being the oldest in a class of younger peers where I felt comfortable and safe to being the youngest in a class of older kids I didn't know. They all had established friendship groups, and there didn't seem to be a place for me.

It was actually a pretty horrible time. No one wanted to sit next to me. No one would partner with me for anything. And I felt lonely, left out, fed up and useless. I didn't know the answers to the questions in class any more as they were all a year ahead of me. So a lot of the time I felt foolish, stupid and inadequate.

All in all, it was a pretty uncomfortable time, and the following year I was very happy to be moved back down again. This was definitely what I wanted and I was glad to be back where I felt more comfortable. But of course, my peers had all experienced a year without me, so once again, friendship groups were pretty set and I was even more of an outsider.

So I carried on as Lone Wolf and convinced myself that I didn't care.

There were definitely times when I just wanted to be accepted and embraced and feel normal - whatever that was! The times when I was accepted into the fold and the girls seemed to like me were nice, and I liked that feeling for a while. But somehow I always felt very different, as if I didn't fit, and it would reach a point where I couldn't bear being around them any longer. They irritated me, got on my nerves, and being my mother's daughter I couldn't hide that irritation!

There was one place in the world where I did feel loved, accepted, and safe. My mother's parents lived in Minehead and we visited Grandma and Pop at least a couple of times a year. I loved it there and quite often it was just me, my mum and sisters that went. Dad stayed behind in Ruislip because of his work, which as far as I was concerned was great. The journey down was always better without him, less stressful and peaceful without the screaming and shouting about getting lost, or swearing at the other idiot drivers on the road. But even when he did come with us he was always on his best behaviour in front of my Grandma and Pop. He wanted their approval so he was always charming and calm and nice in front of them, which meant I could just relax and enjoy being there.

My Grandma was a sweet, kind lady who always smelt of lavender. She was calm and gentle and never shouted at me. Grandma had little whiskers on her chin, and lovely soft hands. She always wore an apron and slippers, and made us junket with cinammon sprinkled on it for pudding.

She used to let me feed Richard and Lucy, their two beautiful tabby cats. I would carefully cut their raw meat into bite sized pieces, put the saucers down on the red stone tiles in the kitchen and watch them eat.

Pop was a little bit intimidating, he didn't smile a whole lot and had great big bushy scratchy whiskers. But he used to take us walking on North Hill with Andy the dog and at night he would sit on my bed and read me bedtime stories using funny voices which made me laugh. I felt safe with Pop.

Wow... thinking and writing about my lovely grandparents brings back some beautifully warm and fuzzy memories and I feel very lucky to have had these kind people in my life. They both died the year I was 13 within eight weeks of each other and I was very sad to lose them.

Interestingly, my father chose that particular time to tell mum that he had fallen in love and was having an affair. Devastating news as you can imagine. My poor mother lost both her parents within weeks of each other, and then my father ripped her world apart even further. I use the word interestingly because I feel there was a subtle reasoning behind his timing. Mum was vulnerable, raw, grieving, and so maybe would not be able to absorb his news easily or stand up to him, which made her more easy to manage and manipulate.

Not long after he broke this news to her I found mum's diary. She had written her thoughts and feelings in a notebook which I accidentally picked up when looking for some note paper, and was I incredibly shocked to read that my father had another woman. It was really awful reading about my mother's confusion and unhappiness. She always seemed so strong, so composed, so unemotional. And now I was seeing her in a different light, aware of her vulnerability, her sadness. Mum soon realised that I knew what was going on, and began to confide in me. I remember feeling so angry on her behalf, and I wanted to hurt him like he was hurting her. I had discovered the name of the woman he was seeing, and one night at the dinner table, I mentioned her name. He looked up as if he had been shot. I glared at him, but didn't have the nerve to say anything directly to him, so I just went on to tell my sisters there was a girl in my class with a horrible, common name, the sort of name a person who cleaned toilets might have. I do recall that he interrupted and tried to say it was a nice name, but I sneered at him and carried on being unkind. I remember how satisfied and delighted I felt to see the hurt look on his face.

What a small, sad victory in the war of painful feelings and unhappiness.

The next few years were pretty difficult at home as his temper worsened and his destructive outbursts increased.

Aged 15 I decided I'd had enough, and ran away to Edinburgh with my mate Sue. Using money I had stolen from my fathers pockets, I bought two train tickets and off we went. I had no fear at all, this was an adventure, and better than being at home with him. Of course there was another rather attractive factor about going all the way to Edinburgh. Our favourite pop group, the Bay City rollers lived in and around the city, and I was certain we would be able to find them. No, don't ask me how - I was just convinced that somehow we would track them down.

I did feel sad about leaving my sisters and mum though, and I really believed I wouldn't see them again for a very long time. So I wrote them a letter from the station before we boarded the train.

Years later my mother gave the letter back to me, along with a little slip of paper with the words "Alive and Well" written next to a name and a phone number of an organisation that provided support for parents if a child had gone missing. There was also a photo of me that she had given to the police. I do recall being pretty disgusted at her photo selection - to be fair it was not one of my better shots! But more to the point was the fact that it had been taken at least four years before, when I was about 11! At the age of 15 I looked very different with my contact lenses in place of the glasses - and thank goodness I had sorted out that unbelievable fringe thing that I had going on!!

* * *

Dear Mum,

Sorry about this, but as you know, I was so sick of Ruislip and everything. Don't think that is was you who made me leave because you had nothing to do with it, except nearly make me change my mind and stay. Me and Sue just want to sort things out. Don't worry about me, cause I am fine, I'm 15 and I know how to look after myself, and you know that I'm not exactly stupid. And don't worry about us becoming prostitutes like that girl in the paper. We're not that dumb. So mum, once again, please <u>don't </u>worry, and don't forget that I love you very much, and Jenny and Alison too. Tell them I love them, and say be good. You can tell Dad what you like, I don't really care.

I'll write again soon, and let you know how I am, and what I'm doing. And above all, <u>don't worry</u> about me, I'm fine, really I am. Anyway, I'll see you soon,

All my love, Marion

ps Tell Rastus and the rest I love them too. Bye for now. I love you all.

* * *

Well, my great adventure ended just one week later when we ran out of money and Sue wanted to come home because she was hungry. I was totally gutted as I really didn't want to go home, but felt I had no choice. So we went to the police station and gave ourselves up.

When I arrived home I was honestly expecting a great welcome - but it was as if I'd only been gone for an hour. I discovered that mum hadn't even told my father I had run away, she said I was staying with a friend and I think she just hoped that I would be back before he noticed how long I'd been gone and finally asked where I was. Mum told me she had to pay for my train ticket home and it would come out of my pocket money for the next few months until it was repaid.

So there I was, back in Ruislip and my father was none the wiser about my adventures. But I guess he was just completely focused on his affair. I later discovered that he told mum he was apparently wrestling with his feelings, his conscience, his morals, and he wanted her to encourage him to stay by being nicer to him. But at the same time he also made it clear that he felt unable to stop seeing the other woman. One evening I remember my mother phoning this woman in desperation, I actually listened to the call. She begged the woman to stop seeing him, telling him that our family was suffering and pleading with her to let him go.

But the woman said she loved him too much and couldn't give him up.

So the affair continued, and after four more years of emotional turmoil and heartache, my mother finally couldn't stand any more and told him he had to leave.

So he moved out and went to live with his new family.

I'm sure his new partner was happy to finally have what she wanted, but I also think she may have got more than she bargained for. Many years later we discovered that her two little girls lives had mirrored ours in more ways than one. They may have got a new father, with his money and jolly demeanour, but as they grew up they also got the anger, the rages, and the abuse.

And so, an uneasy calm descended upon our home in Orchard Close, although a houseful of pubescent and prepubescent teenagers didn't exactly equal calm! Added into the mix was the fact that we were all deeply affected by what had happened and were coping with the fall out, so mum had her hands full trying to manage us all, whilst coping with her own feelings as well.

So this was my childhood.

I don't and can't speak for my sisters because their experiences and memories are different to mine in so many ways.

But for me this is how I feel and remember it. Yes, there were difficult times, scary times, unhappy times. But it wasn't all bad, there were lots of good times too.

Summer holidays, days out, family time spent together. We lived in a lovely area in nice home with a garden, a paddling pool, a summerhouse. We never went hungry.

We had pets, pocket money, presents at Christmas and birthdays.

And we had each other. We may not have appreciated each other fully then, but we do now. My sisters are two of the most important people in my life and I love them deeply.

And here's the thing.

The choices I made, the path I took, the mistakes I made were undoubtedly affected by my childhood. Of course they were. We are all affected by our childhood experiences, the things that happen in our formative years. It's when we learn the most, form our beliefs, and become who we are.

But after all these years, all the learnt behaviours, the wrestling with my demons - I finally choose see it differently.

Oh, for quite a few years I did blame my parents, and felt very resentful towards them.

But they were shaped and formed by their childhoods, their birth order, their own life experiences, just as I have been. They were who and what they were. And then they became my parents and passed on those experiences to me. I am who and what I am now because of those experiences, as are we all.

We all have our imprints from the experiences we had as children, the things that shaped us, the fears we felt and habits that we formed.

And as we grow up we still find ourselves in situations that can be affected by what we learned and dictates our reactions.

But maybe as we mature and become more aware of this we can rationalise it better and deal with feelings and situations differently instead of reacting in the same old ways. We can push out of our comfort zones, take a deep breath, feel the fear, but approach things differently because we know we aren't the scared child any more. Even if we might feel like it. We are now grown ups and can cope better.

So, after years of shame, blame, guilt and anger I wanted to choose something different.

I choose to remember all the good bits and let the rest go

Both of my parents have passed on now, but when I think about them I can see a picture of them in my mind. They are standing together, looking younger than I remember them to be, and they are holding hands and smiling at each other. They are my mum and my dad. And they made me. And in their own ways, they loved me. It wasn't perfect, but it was my life, my childhood, my family, and I am me because of it all.

* * *

I read this positive affirmation somewhere one day, and loved it so much I had to put a copy here for you:

I have a choice, each and every single day.
I choose to feel blessed.
I choose to feel grateful.
I choose to be excited
I choose to be thankful
I choose to be happy.

* * *

And every day I have that choice. The alternative is to carry on being negative, to carry on feeling sorry for myself, to carry on avoiding taking responsibility for myself… And I don't see that as much of a choice!

My parents, my childhood, my many life lessons have enabled and empowered me to become the person I am, and I'm happy and grateful for that.

I can't go back and change anything that happened. So I choose to accept it, and believe it was meant to be.

Because the alternative is to waste my precious time and energy thinking about something that I can have no influence over now. History - or herstory - is exactly that. Yes, it's my story but it's in my past and I don't have the power to change it, even if I wished to. But what I do have is the power to change my attitude, let go of the negatives and not let my life today be affected by the past.

And breathe…!!!

So going back to my story, as you might expect I was your classic rebellious teenager, I didn't want to follow the rules, school was boring and pointless and really only a place to meet my mates, and chat up boys.

As I reached my teenage years I had finally stopped beating the boys up and started falling madly, deeply and passionately in love with one after another of the spotty, immature, foolish creatures. Underneath all that anger, I had a passionate heart, and I wanted a boyfriend. However, I often had trouble finding one. Aged 13, I had virtually reached my full adult height of 5 feet 9 inches (that's 175cm to the converted). And then there were the platform shoes. Oh yes, the seventies were the era of the original platform shoes, and my favourite pair had six inch heels with a four inch wedge. How on earth I ever walked in them is beyond me!

So there I was, a dedicated follower of current fashion, but at 6 ft 3 a head and shoulders taller than all the boys. They would have had to stand on a chair to be anywhere near tall enough to kiss me.

And I wanted to be kissed. I really, really wanted to be kissed.

Kissing was such a romantic thing and proof of a boys love for you. I was twelve when I had my first kiss and it was a good one! The boy's name was John and he kissed me in the bushes outside drama club.

Oh I loved that kiss! It made my toes curl, my tummy flip over, and my heart beat loudly in my ears. I dreamed about it for weeks. I knew that I was in love, and hoped that he loved me too. And I couldn't wait for it to happen again.

But then the next time we kissed he tried to put his hand inside my top and undo my trousers. I was totally mortified. I thought he loved me and wanted me to be his girlfriend, so what was he up to? I had a very limited understanding of sex, my mother hadn't explained much at all, and I wasn't sure what you were or weren't supposed to do with boys.

But in my mind I had worked out that boys asked 'nice' girls out because they wanted to be in a relationship with them, and they didn't do 'that sort of thing' to them. So clearly something was wrong. Obviously, I wasn't viewed as a nice girl, or good enough for girlfriend material. I was something else, although I wasn't sure exactly what at that point. But I didn't like how it felt. So I didn't get to kiss John again and I didn't get a boyfriend. All very disappointing, but I couldn't let my feelings show could I? So here was yet another thing to not feel I was good at, or good enough, and to be angry about.

But it wasn't long before I found something that made me feel better. My cousin Susan introduced me to alcohol at a family wedding. She gave me some lovely sweet cider and I got drunk for the first time. I remember sitting under a table drinking and giggling with Susan and feeling very daring. I liked being naughty like this, and I liked the feeling the cider gave me.

After the wedding reception we had to get the train home, and my father was his usual aggressive and bullying self, shouting at us all to hurry up and get on the train. But now it didn't bother me, I just couldn't care less. I was in a lovely drunken haze where everything seemed so funny, and his bad mood and ill temper washed right over me. And I liked it.

* * *

This is how I remember my first experience with alcohol:

"That misty place I go to inside my head...
treacle and honey and sweet sticky things are there...
ticking time slows down, stops running, just plods along ...
light fading a little...
faces and people become comfortably fuzzy...
dim and distant, mumbling and muzzy...
Feel the friendly, soothing stroke of the see-saw-hee-haw voice...
volume turned down, muted, no sound...
I nod along, just bob along,
and shake my head to the rhythm and beat of the train
As I watch the big red tongue flapping up and down...
see the big red face stretching and shining...
the big red eyes blinking and winking...
Ha ha I can't hear you, I can't feel you...
You can't reach me here, in my woozy, boozy, snoozy world..."

* * *

So from that day on I would regularly pinch money from my Dad's trouser pockets so I could buy alcohol. I'd meet up with my mates and buy cider and pomagne, along with a packet of ten number 6 cigarettes. Oh I was so baaad, and cool! In fact, I would risk or do anything, and I loved to impress my mates. When I was fourteen I decided it would be a good idea to get a tattoo. Of course, good decision, why not?! So I paid £3 to have a butterfly on my right arm which I then had to hide from my father for the next two years for fear he would kick my backside.

I was also very confident about going to go the pub on my own even as young as thirteen. I had to go alone because none of my mates looked old enough! I used to go to the White Swan in Ruislip where I would drink as much vodka and lime as I could afford, as well as anything the locals in there would occasionally buy me. I really can't ever remember anyone asking me how old I was. They didn't ask for ID back then, I was tall, looked older than I was, so they served me. Unbelievable really when you think about it.

And amazingly, my mother never seemed to notice when I came home drunk. I can remember her being very cross one night when I vomited vodka and orange (I was obviously having a change from vodka and lime that night!) all over my new bedroom carpet, but I don't think she ever made the connection and realised I was drunk. Or if she did, she never said so.

I was clever enough at school, in fact I was very intelligent. I passed my eleven plus with flying colours (yes - eleven plus! If you haven't heard of it, google it) and was offered a place at Vyners Grammar School. It was a great opportunity as Vyners was a very good school. I started off pretty well but after the first year I hadn't really made any friends and didn't like the school much at all. I didn't apply myself sufficiently, and when I started going down the pub, homework took something of a back seat.

After three years at Vyners, Mum realised that I wasn't happy there and arranged for me to move to the local secondary school where all my mates went. She made me promise that I would work harder and behave, but unfortunately, I didn't keep that promise. I focused on finding a boyfriend (luckily by now they were getting a bit taller) and entertaining my mates by playing the fool and showing off.

I did love English lessons, I enjoyed writing poetry and stories. But mostly I was disconnected, disengaged, and before I was able to sit my exams a rather unfortunate incident occurred, and I was politely asked to leave the school and not return. So no qualifications for me then!

Out into the big wide world of work, I moved from job to job, never lasting long in any one position. At sixteen my first proper job was in a department store in my local high street. My period of employment lasted four whole days. They sacked me on the Friday because I hadn't returned to work after lunch the day before. I'd stayed in the pub chatting up some builders. I was quite shocked when I arrived at work the next morning and they sacked me, it had all seemed perfectly reasonable to me.

Of course, my lifestyle didn't really make me reliable or capable of focusing on work, a career. I ricocheted from one job to another, often getting the sack because I didn't bother to turn up, or was late, or under the influence of something. I found marijuana, and then speed. I liked speed because it suppressed my appetite, so I took quite a lot of the little blue pills and stayed up all night drinking and partying.

Over the next couple of years I worked in various pubs, restaurants and shops, and even in a residential home for the elderly. Until finally I somehow miraculously secured the position of manager in a doughnut shop. Good old Dougalls Donuts in Uxbridge. I quite liked working there. and I stayed there for a whole year. But despite the blue pills I still ate too many doughnuts, gained two stone in weight and decided I had no option other than to leave before I grew even fatter. So now unemployed, still drinking too much, still angry with life. And to top it off now I was overweight too. Marvellous.

* * *

When I was miserable I often wrote poetry to express how I felt. I'm not sure exactly when I wrote this desperate little ditty, but I found it in an old folder with some photos, and it really sums up how I felt for many years of my life.

Fat, miserable girl
In a world that is
A cholesterol nightmare
Mountains of calories
Towering on the supermarket shelf
Silently calling
'Buy me, eat me'
Turn on TV - what do I see?
Adverts for Pizzas, burgers, Ice cream,

As I munch and crunch
cardboard crispbread and flaccid lettuce,
Boring, tasteless crap.
Enough is enough
I can stand no more
I must have something
To fill the aching void
Inside me
And then the fat cells
Increase again
Flabby, floppy body
Crammed full of junk
Belly bulging....

so the diet starts again tomorrow and

tomorrow and tomorrow and tomorrow....

* * *

Fuelled by anger and alcohol (and clearly too many doughnuts) I found myself in trouble more than once and managed to acquire a criminal record.

And then one more drunken night out resulted in another arrest for stealing thirty bottles of wine and champagne from a restaurant. Crazy behaviour - what was I doing? I had no idea, I was out of control, lost and spinning...

Until finally, shockingly, at the age of 21 I stood before a magistrate and was given a three month custodial sentence.

I couldn't believe it. Were they mad? How could this be happening to me?

But it was. I was sent to Pucklechurch Remand Centre in Bristol, and it was quite honestly one of the most terrifying experiences of my life. I had little or no personal power, couldn't make choices for myself, couldn't remove myself from the danger I felt on a daily basis. The first night sitting in my cell was an incredibly dark moment. I felt as if I were on the edge of a cliff and about to fall off, or maybe I was going to jump. Time dragged by as if with lead weights on its feet, and I found myself in a seriously scary place.

The shame of my mother having to come and visit me there was crushing. I remember sitting across from the table in the visitors room and looking at her face. She was tired and drawn, having driven many miles to see me, but she was there - for me. She was a shining star, writing me letters virtually every day, and those letters meant the world. When you are locked up so many hours a day, the world slows down at times and almost stops, and the boredom is unbearable. But worst of all is all the time you have to think - it's like a rat in your brain, eating away at you, going round and round in circles, over the same thoughts again and again. So I really treasured my mother's letters

And although there were lighter moments, like my easy job in the officers canteen, and my sweet cellmate Cathy, I can honestly say that being in prison was one of the worst times of my life. So many of the women I met in there seemed so detached, disengaged from real life - they were so calm and casual about where they were, almost seemed to enjoy it. But the majority of them were persistent offenders and had been in and out most of their lives. The other women who in for the first time like myself and Cathy were kind of in shock, it was almost like living in a dream. Well, clearly more like a nightmare, and I promised myself that I would never go back. I remember chatting with a prison officer one day as I was mopping the floor, and telling her that I couldn't wait to get out of there and I would not be back. She just laughed and said 'Oh you'll be back, you all are'.

I was outraged, how dare she?! What did she know about me? I wasn't like all the rest, I was different, and once I got out, I was *never* coming back.

Finally, my release date arrived, and I stepped out of Pucklechurch prison armed with my firm resolve to never go back. My mother and sisters came to pick me up, and I felt almost dizzy with relief to be out. My first night of freedom was inevitably spent in the pub with my sisters, tasting my first alcohol for months, and I celebrated the fact that I had survived and was leaving Pucklechurch far behind me forever.

Until I was arrested for shoplifting at Sainsburys three weeks later. Ummm, yes. Arrested again. Within three weeks. As the police interviewed me, the hideous realisation crashed in that the prison officer had probably been right. I was on my way back to prison.

Well you may be forgiven for asking - what on earth was I doing? If I had hated prison so much, and was determined not to go back, why the hell would I be so stupid? Hadn't I learned my lesson? Was I completely deranged?

Well, at that point I couldn't have given you - or myself - an answer. Because I just didn't know. I was completely devastated, convinced I was going straight back to jail, do not pass go, do not collect two hundred pounds - only this wasn't a game of Monopoly, this was real life. Another prison sentence, and for what? Stealing food that I could have paid for. Was I totally crazy? But there I was, seemingly out of control and I just had no idea why.

However, all I can say is that my Guardian Angel was looking out for me on the day I went back to court. My case was being heard by one of the very few female magistrates on the circuit at that time, and although I had heard bad things about her I realise I was very lucky that day. For some reason, this woman actually took the time to look at my file. I remember her saying that something was going wrong in my life and she wanted to know more. So she assigned me a probation officer, ordered social reports, and set a new court date in one months time.

And that is how I met Bunny Matthews.

Bunny was assigned to be my probation officer, and she took me to her office where I sat down in a chair in front of her desk. She picked up my file, flicked through it, then looked at me and said 'Well Marion, you are quite obviously an intelligent, articulate young woman. Shall we find out why you appear to be intent upon messing up your life?' Time seemed to stand still, and I remember sitting and looking at her with a million thoughts flashing through my mind. Big, bad Marion Wright - lone wolf. Was I really going to open up and talk about myself?

Well, apparently I was, because without even realising I had done it, I opened my mouth and just said 'Yes please.'

That was the starting point. It was the first time I could remember someone really taking in interest in me. In my well being, my life.

Although that's probably rather an unfair statement to make because I'm sure my mother was interested, and loved me. But she didn't know how to connect with me, and I do accept that I was a prickly and difficult wolf at times!

So, it may have been that I was just at a point in my life where I was ready to open up, ready to accept some support. But whatever the reasons, Bunny did it for me.

She listened to me. She asked questions about my life and listened to my answers. She didn't interrupt and tell me what I was doing wrong. She didn't judge me. She just listened. She visited my flat and brought me a pack of cigarettes when she knew I had no money. Bunny really seemed to care about me, and I talked and talked and then talked some more. It was as if the lid had blown off my internal pressure cooker and I could let all the crap out. I told her all about my father's affair, his abuse, his rages, my mothers seeming indifference, their divorce, my feelings of inadequacy, my inability to protect my sisters, my anger, my drinking, the drugs. And it felt incredible to finally let it all out.

A month later we returned to court, and Bunny presented her report to the magistrate. I don't really know exactly what she said in it, but I can guess at most of it, and it saved me going back to jail. By this time, with Bunny's support, I had found a job and was feeling so much more positive about my life. So I was delighted to receive a suspended sentence and that was that. I never looked back. My life of crime was behind me, and I truly felt that I had Bunny to thank for helping me to make positive changes and move forward.

I was so lucky to meet her at that time in my life, and looking back I feel so happy and blessed to receive what I now call the 'Bunny Moment'.

And this had a profound effect on me, far greater than I realised back then.

As time progressed, I found I had a desire to help people, make a difference, find a way to offer something that people needed to make a positive change.

I don't know if you have seen the film or read the book entitled 'Pay it Forward?' It is such a beautiful and meaningful story. A little boy is given a school project that asks each pupil to do something that will make a positive difference to the world. So this child creates a very simple concept. He does three favours for three different people. Three acts of kindness that eventually have a positive impact on their lives. And instead of asking them to pay it back to him, he asks them to 'pay it forward' to three other people. It was that simple, and the knock on effect of all that kindness and positivity created a wave of change across the world.

Well, I strongly believe that there can be a 'Bunny Moment' for everyone in their lives, and I know for sure we all deserve one. I'm positive that connecting with Bunny at such a pivotal time in my life is what has prompted me down my path of working with teens, families, children, vulnerable people. I have a deep desire to pay it forward by creating a 'Bunny Moment'. If I can make a connection with someone in need, someone in pain, someone who maybe feels lost, lonely, desperate, then maybe I can share a few words that may resonate and provide an opportunity for a different and more positive train of thought. Something to maybe spark an idea, to release them from a dark place they have been in, to facilitate positive change. Or maybe it's just something as simple as a smile and a happy greeting. Isn't that a wonderful thing to be able to offer the world?

So, thanks to Bunny, I made it through the dark times, and whilst life didn't suddenly become perfect it definitely improved.

Over the next few years I bought my own flat, worked two jobs to pay for it, and kept my head above water. Of course, I still partied hard and had my moments, but hey, that was me and I was doing alright.

Then at the age of 26 I met my husband to be. I fell instantly, madly in love, and within a year we were married. I quickly had two fabulous children, my daughter Clare who is now 30, and my son Zachary who is 27. They are wonderful, beautiful, unique people, and I adore everything about them.

So there I was, happily married and living the dream with my beautiful family. And when my children were little I decided I wanted to stay at home and be their full time mum. Having finally settled down and worked hard for the past few years I was looking forward to this next stage of my life and just experiencing being mum.

However, financially it soon became clear that this wasn't possible, and I needed to get a job of some description. So after a few months working in a part time clerical position during the evenings, alongside a couple of cleaning jobs, I decided to supplement the family income for the next few years by registering as a child minder.

Now I thought this would be a bit of a doddle, an easy way of making some money whilst my little ones were at home. And although I enjoyed it, I soon came to realise it wasn't quite the easy ride I had imagined. However, it suited me and I was quite good at it.

I also found myself observing and analysing the behaviours of the children in my care, and I started to realise that I had something of a gift for seeing the bigger picture and understanding children's challenging behaviours. I had clear rules and boundaries in my house about what they could and couldn't do, and even though the parents often complained about their kids behaviour at home, when they were at my house they were wonderful! Maybe I just scared them! But in all seriousness I know that wasn't the case, they really enjoyed being there, despite my rules and expectations.

Alongside the child minding I did some training and began working some evenings as a part time youth worker for Northamptonshire Youth Service. It was then that I really discovered my passion for working with and empowering young people. I think that my somewhat misspent youth may well have helped me to understand and empathise with what was going on for many of them! I organised and facilitated girls groups, young mums groups, residential weekends, foreign exchange trips, and loved it all.

I was then seconded to a team working with a new innovation in our area, Out of School support. A large grant from the European Social Fund enabled the new initiative, and the projects were so successful that once the ESF funding ended, the local County Council picked up the funding. Basically, we were spending a couple of days a week with the 'hardcore' students, the ones who caused the most disruption at school. We did a lot of work around social skills, spent time listening to them, and most of them engaged positively and enjoyed their time with us. Before long we were providing full time support to these students, and the project then became a Pupil Referral Unit. I worked my way from Assistant to project Co ordinator - a post which excited and terrified me in equal measures! It was a huge responsibility to try and keep these young people engaged through their last year of formal education, and it seemed that every day brought a new challenge!

The schools were doing their best, but mainstream education just doesn't suit all young people for a variety of reasons, and so Springboard offered something different.

Having received messages indicating that they were lazy, stupid, disruptive, trouble makers from a very early age, these children grew up believing they were no good, and so they set out to try and prove this to be true. Inevitably they had low self esteem, and negative attention for bad behaviour created yet more bad behaviour. They wouldn't conform, or give in, or accept help or advice from their parents, teachers or anyone they regarded in authority.

So there had been this increasing downward spiral as the years went on. The children's behaviour deteriorated, the parents continued to receive negative feedback which they didn't know how to deal with. Consequently they had no faith in themselves as parents and didn't know what to do with their children.

By the time their children came to our project, these parents were pretty fed up. I often found that they hadn't heard anyone say something good about their child for a long time. They were sick of the negativity that seemed to surround their child's educational and social experiences, they saw their kids as failures and felt that they had failed as well.

So it seemed obvious that we needed to work with the parents and carers as well as their children. Clear and frequent communication via letters and phone calls kept them informed of their child's progress and we focused as much on the positive as possible. Of course, there were incidents and challenges and the students had to be given consequences for their actions. And so we would have to tell the parents about this. But we didn't make a drama out of their actions. If they were sent home one day, then once that was done with we welcomed their child back to the project the following day for a fresh start.

And at the end of every week I sent a letter home telling the parents about their child's positive achievements. Because at Springboard we were trying to provide a positive environment, give the teens positive praise and acceptance, along with some nice clear boundaries, rules and consequences.

And they pushed those boundaries every day! Of course they did. They had to keep testing us to see if we meant what we said.

Springboard was a great project. Of course, every day brought something different, a new challenge, but also a new positive achievement.

* * *

Sleep Deprivation

I would just like to take a moment to talk a little about sleep deprivation.

I was incredibly fortunate that both my babies slept through the night from a very early age. Clare was around four weeks, and Zac at about six weeks. And they didn't keep me awake for hours when they were tiny. So I don't know what endless sleepless night look like, and I am extremely grateful for that.

I know! Please don't hate me!

Sleep deprivation seems to be an acceptable part of life nowadays, but did you know that it is actually an *internationally recognised form of torture*?

Lack of sleep is just hugely detrimental to our health. And yet there seems to be a general belief that having a baby will probably result in years of sleepless nights. For some reason, it's just accepted and even expected that babies won't sleep.

Why is this? Babies thrive on sleep. Babies *need* sleep. We all need sleep.

Sadly, we know that health issues such as ADHD are associated with sleep deprivation, and yet it still seems to be acceptable and embraced as the norm and we all just get on with it.

But it doesn't need to be like this. Honestly, babies are designed to sleep and are capable of sleeping for twelve hours through the night, with day time naps as well.

But I am happy to say that luckily there is an excellent, insightful book about baby sleep and associated conditions written by my wonderful sister, Alison Scott-Wright. Quite simply, 'The Sensational Baby Sleep Plan' helps parents to train their babies to sleep through the night. Testimonials from hundreds of her clients talk about the devastating impact that lack of sleep was creating and it's far reaching damaging effects on their family. But with the help of Alison's book they were able to make dramatic improvements and find some balance and harmony - not to mention some sleep!

We all need sleep. Alison says that sleep is the key to life and sleep is not just desirable, but important and necessary for our health and well being.

And I agree. I loathe being tired. I love my sleep! Sleep promotes good health and a positive outlook. It's so much easier to face the day after a good night's sleep.

I certainly saw the effects of sleep deprivation on the students at Springboard. They often arrived looking exhausted before the day had even started properly, saying that they had only had a few hours sleep and been up most of the night on their mobile phones! So how were they expected to focus, concentrate, and learn new information? Let alone function and just get through the day.

So I cannot emphasise enough the importance of sleep.

* * *

I have to say that when I became a mother, I was quite simply terrified. Panic stricken at the thought of the responsibility, the thought of having to take care of a tiny little human being. How could I do this, how could I get it right? Being an oldest child, always wanting to be in control, and something of a perfectionist, as well as being very self critical and terrified of 'failure' I was now in a minefield of risk and fear. What if my beautiful little girl didn't sleep and I couldn't do anything about it? What if she became ill and I couldn't make her better? What if I didn't feed her properly, what if I hurt her, what if I couldn't be good enough? And what if people saw me making mistakes, saw me letting her down, saw me getting it wrong? My youngest sister had a little boy, my sister in law had two and to me it all looked perfect. They seemed capable, happy, relaxed, their children were thriving, sleeping, contented. So now I had to do the same. No pressure then!!

I don't think I relaxed properly for years. Truly, I was always so worried and stressed. And I think that alongside my need to control and be seen as a good mother, there was the spectre of my own difficulties and learnt behaviours from my own my childhood. I existed in a pretty much constant state of not being good enough, and just had to try to prove I was and make everything perfect.

So, how did I deal with this stress and fear? Well, quite simply I became superwoman. I became all things to all people - except of course, myself.

When Clare was only a few months old my husband suggested we move to Northampton to live near his family. As a new mum I was struggling, my confidence was round my ankles and the fact that they wanted to help me such was a relief so it seemed like the best thing to do. I had convinced myself that my mother wasn't particularly interested in my life so I didn't see much of her. My father and I weren't close. Little sister was married with a toddler and living her life, middle sister was single and living the high life in Australia. And I wasn't good at asking for help, or support, or letting them see I couldn't cope.

So without a second thought I agreed to move. I loved my husbands family, they seemed so caring and normal and they seemed to love me too.

But sadly that still wasn't enough for me. I had to keep trying harder and harder to make them love me more, be the very best daughter in law/sister in law/wife/mother/aunt. Quite frankly, it was exhausting, but I couldn't stop. And looking back, what I realise now is that I had no love for myself, and this created the whole searching, yearning need to be the best, and therefore, be seen as loveable.

I didn't have the cape, the tights or the headpiece, but I was definitely Superwoman, and I flew around being wonderful. I helped my mother in law when she became ill and for the next seven years I was there, cleaning, supporting, trying to fix it. My sister in law had her challenges, so I was there as well, cleaning, supporting, baby sitting, trying to fix her life.

I guess by now you can see the pattern emerging! It was all about everyone else. If I was 'helping' other people, I didn't have to think about my own life.

I couldn't risk stopping to think about me, how I felt, what I wanted or needed, because if I did I felt emotions that I didn't like.

The truth was I often felt lonely, scared, isolated, sad, overwhelmed, unworthy, unloved, inadequate...

Oh dear, no, stop right there! I couldn't deal with those feelings at all! So my coping mechanism was to carry on being Superwoman. Helping, doing, running, flying, wearing myself out and becoming more and more stressed, on to the next thing, rushing, never taking the time to stop. Because if I stopped I might let the feelings in, and I just didn't want them or know what to do with them.

And so all of this affected my parenting. Of course it did - how could it not?!

Because in all this rushing around as Superwoman, my children had to try to keep up. If we were going out anywhere I was always stressed. 'Where's the changing bag? Have I got everything? Get your coat on, quickly, come on, gloves, hat, don't be silly, do your shoes up, you know how to do it, we're late, let's go, no we haven't got time to find teddy, hurry, quickly, out the door.' And then there was the minefield of the car seat, the straps and buckles, always so tricky. I would yank and pull and force the buckle in place, muttering under my breath about how difficult it all was, why couldn't it just fit, while my beautiful little children just sat there patiently. And then one day as I was wrestling with the straps once again, my daughter said to me 'Mummy, why do you always put your teeth out at me?'

Whoa there...! What did she mean, why did I put my teeth out at her? And then to my guilt and shame and absolute horror, I realised what she meant. She was seeing me clenching my teeth, frowning, looking fierce and angry and stressed. Just as I used to see my father's face on so many occasions.

She didn't see her mummy taking a moment to look into her beautiful, innocent, trusting eyes and smiling, letting her know that her mummy loved her. Oh no, mummy was too busy rushing around and what my daughter was seeing was Superwoman. But this was stressed, frustrated, angry and put upon Superwoman, the one who 'put her teeth out' at her children, the one behind the scenes, behind the facade.

The front cover of this book is a picture that Clare drew when she was almost four years old. Zac was just thirteen months. It is a bit speckled and dirty because it was on the fridge at home, and over the years as I have moved about, but for some reason it has stayed the course.

Looking at it now I completely understand the picture. The black colouring over my forehead and right eye must have been her seeing me frowning and glaring. Children draw what they see, and I don't think I need say more. It's not the best memory, but I guess what I can do now is appreciate all the lovely rainbow colours and just be thankful that she didn't add a large set of gnashing, snarling teeth!

So, this was the parent my family sometimes saw and heard and lived with, but no one else really did. For the world it was all about keep up the front, keep going, keep making them think I'm wonderful, keep trying to make them love me.

* * *

> Writing these words isn't easy.
>
> Remembering the things I got wrong and the impact on my family is not a good feeling. And over the years, those words from my daughter haunted me. But I had to hear them.
>
> And so finally - deep breath - I choose to look back and forgive myself.
>
> I have to remember that I did my best as the person I was at the time and that is all any of us can ever do.

* * *

But I was starting realise that even though Superwoman continued on her daily quest, I was actually in trouble and not really coping too well. I suffered with pre menstrual stress for around ten days every month which created frightening mood swings. It was pretty awful, but I accepted that this was my life and I just had to get on with it.

Then one day I decided to see my gp. I had a couple of minor issues going on, just routine stuff. The doctor was a very kind, friendly man and before I knew it I started telling him how awful I felt. I knocked a couple of bricks out of my wall, removed my superwoman cape and took the first tentative steps down the road to asking for help.

Looking back, I'm so glad I did! The doctor suggested counselling and to be honest, the way I was feeling I was eager to try anything. I didn't know much about how counselling worked, but when I started I loved it. Being able to tell someone how I felt after all those years was wonderful. It had been a long time since my 'Bunny Moment', and I was ready to talk! It was like there was a filing cabinet, or big cupboard in my mind that had burst open and all the files and stuff were scattered all over the floor in a mess.

But over the next few weeks, with the counsellor's patient support and guidance, I started sorting it all out. I didn't feel judged or criticised, I just felt safe and supported. Of course, it wasn't an instant fix, but it was an amazing feeling and such a relief to start letting some of what had been stored up in my head for years out into the open. Over the weeks I found I was beginning to sort stuff out and create a little order from the mess.

Listen - it was a big job! And I wasn't going to do it all in a few weeks and wave a magic wand and make everything perfect!

But it was my starting point towards learning more about me, my needs and my feelings.

I am eternally grateful to my counsellor she was so skilled at encouraging me to think things through, question my beliefs about my role in my family, helping me to see that there were things that happened I wasn't responsible for and everything wasn't always *all MY fault*! So as time progressed, my life improved and my stress eased a little.

So whilst this was all good and positive, I still felt that at times my parenting skills weren't always the best. My children were wonderful, they slept well, did as they were told, they were cute, loving, polite. They really were gorgeous, funny, sweet little souls, very clever and confident. So I was so very fortunate, but didn't always realise it. I expected a lot from them, and I sometimes became frustrated and angry, shouting and occasionally smacking them.

Well, clearly this was not positive, powerful parenting! And I didn't like myself when I was acting this way, so I signed up for a parenting course.

* * *

And I've just noticed that here's something to really give myself credit for. Looking back over the years I see that when I finally realised that I needed to change something, I wasn't shy or self conscious about finding help. When I was in counselling, when I was in training sessions or on a course I would quite openly admit to my faults and bare my soul in the quest for support and assistance to become better. Great quality Marion - well done! Acknowledgement and praise of the positives and good things is so much better than punishing myself for the mistakes and not so good things!

* * *

And my goodness - talk about life changing! Signing up for that parenting course was the best thing I ever did!

The course facilitator was a wonderful lady named Anna Smith, and her encouragement and support was very empowering. We learnt about positive and responsible parenting, and I actually believe it saved my sanity! Of course, we didn't become perfect parents overnight. No, it took time to make some changes, to form new habits, to practice and remember new approaches, and not revert to our old approach. I didn't get it right all the time, and looking back, I realise that was alright too. Nobody is the perfect parent, not even Superwoman! And what mattered was that I was trying.

Over the next couple of years I signed onto the course five more times. I just felt I was a better parent when I was constantly reminding myself of the things that helped and supported me.

Which was great - for me - and for my family!

So looking back I can see how my parenting approach started to shift and change for the better. I was learning to give positive attention, thinking about responsibility, changing some learnt behaviours. This resulted in me feeling better equipped to cope, more positive about myself as a parent, more empowered.

* * *

Sometimes I look through my memory boxes and find a little treasure. My beautiful, brave daughter wrote this letter to me when she went to live and work in Australia. She was only 17, and travelling across the world on her own. It was hard to watch her go, but wonderful to see her spread her wings and fly with such courage. And her letter reminds me that as a parent I must have done something right!

Dear Mum,

I don't need to explain anything to you because you understand me and why I'm doing this. So all I'll say is I will miss you so much, but I promise you I'm just trying to be happy. I love you Mum, you're my best friend and I want to thank you for being there for me always.

I'll miss our little chats, our in depth conversations - so EMAIL me!! I really will miss you, I hope things at work settle down - or you decide what to do. Keep me updated. I love you and I'm proud of your strength and confidence. Hopefully I'll be that strong one day. Your daughter and best friend, I love you xoxoClarexoxo

As an after thought... This letter and no other could every truly express how much you mean to me, but I hope that you see it in my eyes when I smile, laugh, cry and frown that I'm a younger, not-quite-so-wise, loving caring, smaller version of you, and I'm so proud to be. You're such an inspiration and I don't think I could love you more. See you soon! xoxo

A letter from my girl telling me how much she loved me - and not a mention of the gnashing teeth. Fabulous!

* * *

So, I think that I will stop my story here. Of course there is much more, but in relation to this book maybe you have all you need.

I've learned so much and all these years down the line I want to share this wonderful learning and provide something deeper for parents. Years of my own parenting experiences, but also working with children and teenagers and their families taught me a lot. And I strongly feel that it's no good trying to just fix one area or aspect of our life, we need to look at the big picture, and embrace a holistic approach. It's like a big jigsaw puzzle and we need all the pieces the right way round to create the big picture.

So that's why I decided to write this book.

Quite simply, I believe that the answer is to find belief in ourselves. And learn how to love ourselves. And accept ourselves as the truly wonderful, amazing human beings - and humans doing - that we are.

And *you* are good enough right now.

Accept all that *you* are, all that *you* have done.

You can't change the past, there is only this moment, and then the next.

Keep believing in yourself, keep the faith, keep working on finding that positive approach and you will fly. Not like superwoman, but like the beautiful, deserving, whole and loving person that you already are, but just didn't know it!

I truly hope you enjoy reading this book.

CHAPTER TWO

HAVE FAITH

Having faith in yourself is hugely important. You're not failing, you're not useless, you're just doing your best in a tough old world! And it can be a critical, judgemental, demanding place at times.

Don't forget, parenting is just about the hardest job in the world. It's constant, full on, no tea breaks or days off sick! Not a lot of training, and your child doesn't come with a manual or instructions. We learn our parenting skills from our own parents, who in turn learnt from their own.

So, we're doing our best with what we know, and none of us are deliberately trying to get it wrong and be a 'bad' parent!

The pressure to be a 'good' parent is huge.

(And we will explore the concept of 'good' parenting in chapter four)

It comes from society in general, other parents, family members, peer groups, school. And of course, we judge ourselves most harshly and put the most pressure upon ourselves.

But please take heart, you just need to have a little faith in yourself, your child, and in your ability to be exactly the parent and person you want to be.

Ok, so I hear you ask, just what does this mean? How can we have faith in ourselves when we often *feel* as if we are failing? When we're tired, fed up, demoralised and ground down by hearing:

'I hate you! You're so unfair! You never let me do *anything!* My life is so awful! Why did you even bother to have me? You just don't want me to be happy...'

From your child! The child that was once your cuddly, loving little girl or boy, asking for bedtime stories, holding your hand as you walked them to school. Remember the photos you took of their endless cuteness. Maybe you can remember sometimes creeping into their bedroom at night just to watch them sleep and your heart almost wanting to burst with love and pride and an overwhelming desire to keep them safe forever.

Where did that little person go?

How did it all change?

And what can you do now?

Well, the first thing I want you know is that they are still there. They just get a little bit lost sometimes and so do we.

And please remember that you're not alone. So many parents feel the same, exhausted and fed up with what appears to be a never ending battle. Sometimes it seems that no matter what they do, the bad behaviours and the challenges continue, and it often seems easier to just give in than continue arguing and fighting.

Lets face it, life is like a fishbowl at times. We are under constant scrutiny and pressure and this increases enormously when we have a child. Inevitably we begin to compare ourselves and our baby to others. Right from the word go our parents, family members and friends all have well meaning suggestions and ideas for us. Support is great, advice is great, chatting about your children is great, but when you start to compare you can find yourself doubting yourself, your abilities, and your own instincts.

So as our confidence starts to erode further, we question ourselves, our abilities, our parenting skills, and self doubt creeps in.

Then when they start school, there's another whole area of pressure. Is your child learning as quickly as their peers? Will what you put in their lunch box be frowned upon as unhealthy? Suddenly it seems that people are judging your child's appearance, their behaviour, their progress and consequently you as their parent! It's tough!!

And along with all of this is the monster of social pressure and the media. Does your child attend the right social activities, do they wear the right clothes, have the best stuff? It's a complete nightmare out there for parents with every type of advertising being thrown at you from every direction. There's no escape, it comes via email, pops up on your phone, facebook, tv, newspapers, magazines, you name it, it's there. Not to mention the peer pressure that your child experiences and passes on to you. How many times do you hear 'everyone else is going, everyone else has one, everyone else is wearing it...?!' And it's so hard to deny them.

Years pass by, you keep working to put food on the table, buy the latest gadgets, pay for school trips, holidays, birthdays, christmas.

It's no wonder you can end up tired, knackered, worn out, and sometimes feeling as if you are buried underneath a mountain of guilt, inadequacy, debt and fear.

So, I ask again, what can you do? Well, part of the answer may actually be simpler than you thought.

Your child behaves and responds as well as you allow them to.

Yes of course they will try to convince you that they need you to buy them the latest gadgets, or let them stay out until midnight on a school night. They are children, and it's their job to push us to the limit!

But the truth is that actually they look for guidance and strength from you, and are often only responding to what you give them.

If you come from a negative place they will respond negatively.

If you have given up before you start, then they will always win.

If you are anticipating and expecting there to be problems, then there will be problems.

And if you don't mean what you say, they can't trust you and will question *everything!*

The answer is in you, it's all in you, you had it all along, but it's been buried deep beneath your fears.

And I know that those fears are very real, created by our doubts about ourselves as a person, let alone as a parent to a child.

But again, you are truly not alone! So many other parents feel the same way as you do on some level, battling with the same self doubt, guilt, and fear. Many of them lack belief in their abilities, believe they are 'failures', become tired, overwhelmed, demoralised.

And don't forget, just because we become a parent, we don't automatically shrug off all our 'stuff'. We are still stuck with our insecurities, our history and herstory. Those family experiences, the habits and learnt behaviours from the way we were parented. The often unresolved feelings from our experiences as children.

So there we are, going through life coping with all that in our own now grown up lives, and then we become a parent! Suddenly we aren't just responsible for our own lives, we now have small people relying on us too. Tiny little fragile people we love and adore with all our hearts. They are depending on us to attend to their needs, nurture and care for them and make sure we get it right. They grow into toddlers who seem to start to challenge our every word, and then children with changing needs and requirements and an answer for everything, and then hostile, uncommunicative teens!

Without a doubt, the pressure increases. Sometimes, molehills become mountains, many situations seem insurmountable, and nothing goes right. So you reach a point where you end up at a complete loss to know what to do next because it seems you have tried everything and failed. The only thing to do is keep plodding on, hoping something will change.

Understandably, there is a temptation to make like an ostrich at times, stick your head in the sand and just hope it will all go away or magically get better!

Oh, trust me, we've all been there - head down, bum in the air, pretending there's nothing wrong and hoping for a miracle!

But the trouble is, it doesn't really work does it?

Sometimes it goes quiet for a while, no major dramas are occurring and you desperately hope things just might be improving. So you risk taking your head out of the sand and then - BOOM - something kicks off so it starts up all over again and the cycle continues.

So you give yourself an even harder time and end up feeling worse. Tiredness and exhaustion because of all the worry and stress builds. It can start to feel like you're buried under a mountain of worry and fear and have absolutely no idea what to do next. Well, what *can* you do next?!

Well, as a great starting point, why not listen to some Meatloaf?!

There's a great line in one of my favourite Meatloaf songs that goes :

'STOP RIGHT THERE!!'

And quite seriously, this is what you need to do. Just stop for a moment or two. Put it all on hold. Take a step back, take some time for yourself without anyone else around. Sit down somewhere quiet, and make sure you're comfortable. Give yourself some breathing space. Take a deep breath, a nice slow inhalation of breath, and let it out very slowly. Then take a couple more like that. No heaving and whooshing and panting, just long slow healing breaths that fill your lungs, your belly, all of your body, and then exhale slowly and steadily. Oh, and yes, let your belly stick out! Especially if you are a woman, don't worry about trying to hold it in, we are meant to have rounded bellies we are females we are feminine we are beautiful women! And we have beautiful rounded bellies!

So now check where your shoulders are. You'll probably find that they are tucked up under your ears where they've pretty much taken up permanent residence! Let them drop, wriggle them about a bit, try to relax as much as you can.

Now you've done that, you can stop and have a look at where you are and what is going on. Really take a good long, hard, honest look.

Be brave, because it may all look and feel a bit daunting, frightening, terrifying even.

But here is where you reassure yourself that this is the moment it can all start to improve.

Right here is where you can start to change the process.

Right now is where you can start to do it differently.

Look at this way, why not have a go at making a change? What have you got to lose?

You've been going round in the circles, you've worried yourself sick, you feel you've tried everything, and it's all still the same.

So now, instead of telling yourself how hopeless it all is, and how useless you are, how much you've failed, do something different!

The first thing to do is stop worrying about what has happened in the past because you can't change any of it now. Wouldn't it be great if we were all born with a handy remote control? How wonderful to be able to pause, or freeze, or press catch up for the bits we might have missed, or rewind to a point where we could have made different decisions and choices.

But there's no remote is there? And so every single thing that happened ten minutes ago, ten days ago, ten weeks ago, ten years ago is all gone. Finished, done, gone, and you can't do anything about it now.

You will have made mistakes. You will have experienced sad times and bad times. You will more than likely be living with feelings of guilt or regret about decisions you made, opportunities you missed, or be wishing you could change certain things. But you can't, and it's the now you have to focus on.

Do you remember what good old Forrest Gump said? 'Life is like a box of chocolates, you never know what you're gonna get.'

And once the box is open, you will find delicious flavours that you love, some that you can't stand, maybe a rock hard toffee that breaks your tooth! But when it's open, you won't be able to take it back and change all the ones you don't like. You have to put up with them don't you? And in the same way, life is made up of lovely bits, joyful bits, sad bits, frightening bits, bits that make you want to just curl up into a ball and hide. And then there are the bits that make you want to scream from the rooftops from sheer exhilaration and excitement.

Nothing is ever wonderful all the time, and we can't get it right all the time either. So once it's done, gone, and in the past then try to learn from it and then let it go.

And yes, I know this might be easier said than done! It takes effort and practice and a new, awakened awareness to try to change the old habits, but *is* possible. Stop revisiting the past, because it truly is a pointless exercise of wasted energy and wasted time, and you really don't have that energy to waste! What you are going to focus on is the right here and now and start making positive changes that will benefit and positively affect you in this moment and then the next.

So, let's get back to making it happen.

Next thing to do is to kick all the mental nagging, the negative thoughts, the constant shame and blame into touch. Yes, yes, I know that again this can be easier said than done, but you have to start somewhere, so why not here and now?

It's massively important that you stop giving yourself a hard time.

Stop listening to the poison parrot voice in your head that tells you:
Squawk - you aren't good enough!
Squawk - you let everyone down!
Squawk - you're a failure!
Squawk - you deserve to feel guilty!
Squawk - LOSER!

No, you've listened to old poisoned polly for long enough, and where has it got you? Enough is enough. It's time to make a change because all those negative words don't help us at all. When we receive negative messages, no matter where from, it doesn't make us feel good. In fact, it's very damaging, and the more we hear the more we believe it and the worse we feel. We all know that if children hear negative messages they are more likely to grow up with low self esteem. And it's no different for us as adults. We need to hear positive messages that will make us feel good about ourselves, not worse.

So if all you are doing is verbally beating yourself up, that is just not going to help in any way, and in fact is just more damaging for you.

What you *can* do is focus your precious energy on creating positive changes in the now, this moment, and in the moment after that. And you're going to take it breath by breath, step by step, day by day. And the very important thing is, you're going to support and look after yourself while you do it.

Take a few moments to sit and think about all the hard work you put in every single day. Remind yourself you are doing your best. Focus on what you have done well, and think about the positive achievements that you *do* make, all the time. I mean, come on, it's pretty amazing that throughout your day you put food on the table, do the washing, go to work, or work at home, help someone with their homework, call your mum, feed the cat, walk the dog, take the kids to ballet, wash the car... you really don't need me to go on do you? Without a doubt, all of these are positive achievements. So recognise this and praise yourself. And you will feel stronger and more able to keep going if you *look after yourself too*!

Find faith and belief in yourself. Find your positive power and make it happen

Focus your energy on positive outcomes, believe that things will get better, and little by little they will.

And one step at a time really is the way forward. Don't expect massive changes straight away. It may take a little time and practice to get this new attitude going, and you may well take a step forward, and then one back again. But this is just how life goes, and it doesn't mean you're failing again or doing it all wrong. You're an amazing human being, and an amazing human doing your best, and that is good enough. Just imagine that you're doing a little dance through life, step forward, step back, shake your hips, cha cha cha!!

You can do this. And now is as good a time to start as any!

Your Golden Rule

If you focus on the negative, and expect the negative, then that's what you will probably get. The power of positive thinking is phenomenal, so make it work for you. Start small, work on one thing at a time, have faith in a positive outcome and see what happens. Then you can tackle the next thing, and before you know it, you are standing in your positive power and life is getting better and better. One breath, one step, one day at a time!

Your moment of sunshine

Laugh! Find something to laugh at in your day. Don't be so serious! I'm sure you've heard the saying, we only get this one life, and it's not a rehearsal? Make it count, make it fun, do your very best to enjoy it. Watch a funny film. Play a game. Have joke time with the children. (watch it with the teens though, I'm sure they will tell jokes that make your toes curl!!) Think of something or someone that makes you smile. Laughing and smiling releases those good old happy hormones, and makes us feel a whole lot better.

———⊂≣≣≣⊃———

Reminding you that you are good
enough exactly as you are

* * *

And Faith was good enough exactly as she was, in fact she was perfect.

I met Faith and her parents in the Dominican Republic a few years ago. Faith was five years old, and I discovered that she couldn't see or hear, nor could she speak. Faith was a chinese orphan who had been adopted by two lovely people who I will call Jane and Anthony. As we stopped for lunch I felt so drawn to Faith that I deliberately made sure I sat next to her. She must have felt a presence and she turned towards me, and reached out her hand to touch mine. She started stroking and feeling my hand, intently absorbing the sensation whilst smiling quietly to herself. After lunch she stood up and started to walk away from the table. I got up to follow her, concerned that she might bump into something. But Jane said Faith would be fine. So I watched her move away from us, and it was just as if she were floating. Her hands were outstretched, her arms waving gently around as if in a beautiful dance. She appeared to be feeling her way, sensing obstacles in front of her without touching them, and she just moved round them. It was beautiful watching her holding her face to the warm breeze, inhaling, smelling, tasting the air. She looked tranquil and balanced and as if she were truly sensing and absorbing everything around her.

Watching this tiny girl just being who she was, enjoying the simplest things made me feel very humble. We are so incredibly blessed to have the things we tend to take for granted and we often feel sadness for someone who appears 'disabled' or impaired in any way. Not quite complete. Not quite 'normal.' Oh how I dislike that word! Normal? Define normal for me please!

This little girl was perfectly complete in her own way. Life was different for her, but who is to say it was diminished or worse? We've been trained to believe that if we don't have good physical health, all our senses, all our fingers and toes, then we are lacking something.

Well as far as I could see, Faith lacked nothing. She was loved, cared for, encouraged, and nurtured. She was breathing, feeling, absorbing and enjoying life her way.

Faith moved me deeply, and I was inspired to write this tribute to her.

Do we have Faith in our hearts, is Faith filling our lives?
Do we want Faith to release us from our troubles and strife?
Is it Faith that moves mountains, is it Faith that parts seas?
Can Faith strengthen your soul when you're brought to your knees?

Can Faith feed the hungry, does Faith give to the poor?
Can Faith heal all our sickness, bring an end to all wars??
Does Faith create love and can Faith erase doubt?
And is Faith the strength that casts all hatred out?

If it is, then what is Faith - where can it be found...?
In the air, in the sea, in the clouds, in the ground..?
Is it sunshine or raindrops, a stone or a feather?
Can we touch it and hold it and keep it forever?

Or is the answer quite simple, is it there for us all, shall we
open our hearts and tear down our high walls?
Practice love and acceptance and just letting go of
resentment and judgement, our shame and our woes

Take the labels of boxes and embrace the unique,
Celebrate what is different, give our love to the weak,
Offer food to the hungry, a guiding hand to the lost...
Does a smile, a soft touch, a kind word really cost?

Don't be shy - Faith is coming, shall we open our minds?
Don't be timid - be bold, and in our our hearts we will find
that Faith is within us, and it was there all along,
true belief, complete trust, and intuition that's strong

I found that the beauty of Faith is a five year old girl,
who is bringing a message that needs to be heard,
Faith was hidden and voiceless, trapped behind a great wall,
this small child, this huge spirit, this great gift to us all

Faith moves through this world with no sight, and no sound,
but she flows and she dances, feet firm on the ground.
Faith twisting and turning and touching and tasting,
her senses in tune with this world, nothing wasted.

Through love, she has freedom, she's thriving and growing,
flickering, shimmering, shining and glowing,
Faith dances in the sunlight, Faith sings her own songs
in a world where she counts, a world where she belongs

Starfish hands floating, and whispering fingers
that curl around your heart, and the feeling that lingers
is of ancient wisdoms, innate knowledge, and hope,
hope for us as the ones that sometimes fumble and grope

In our own lives of darkness where we don't always listen,
to ourselves, to each other, we ignore tears that glisten,
we forget what we value, we don't know where to go…
We lose sight, we lose heart, we lose Faith - until now.

* * *

Acceptance And Acknowledgment

Acceptance is immensely, incredibly important.

Acceptance of ourselves, acceptance of each other, acceptance of the diversity and differences in the world.

And acceptance of the fact that we all make mistakes!

Mistakes don't mean it's the end of the world, or that we can never put anything right, or that we're bad people.

We're human beings, and we're humans doing our best.

We're not perfect and we don't know it all. Every day of our lives is an opportunity for a new lesson, a new experience, a new challenge. So how on earth can we get everything right all of the time?

Well quite simply, we can't. It's impossible, so we need to accept that and stop trying to make it all perfect.

Life is just about doing your best.

Do your best to get up when you fall, dust yourself off and carry on.

Do your best to keep listening and learning and trying.

Do your best to accept who you are, be proud of who you are, and have some appreciation for the wonderful person that you are.

Self improvement is a very wonderful thing, but so is self acceptance.

Be kind to yourself.

Accept and love and approve of yourself right now, exactly as you are and set yourself free from guilt, fear and blame.

There is a wonderful saying that goes something like this:

> **Please grant me the serenity to accept the things I cannot change, the courage to change the things I can, and the wisdom to know the difference.**

Well as we know, everything is open to interpretation. But I believe that this may be what it means:

Accept the things I cannot change

Well, this takes us back to what we read at the end of the 'Have Faith' section. You can't change the past, so try to accept it and don't fight it. Also, it's about the present moment, and learning to accept ourselves the way we are, other people for who they are, and not constantly striving and struggling to change ourselves or them.

Have the courage to change the things I can

In this moment, and the next. The decisions and choices you make now will affect your future so have courage and make the best ones possible even if they seem hard at the time. We can often feel as if we don't have a choice but we usually do. However it often doesn't feel that way because we don't like our options and the choice may be difficult to make. It may push us outside our comfort zone or seem impossible to do so we don't consider it choice.

Grant me the wisdom to know the difference

Maybe part of accumulating wisdom is about learning from mistakes, learning what to expend your energy on and what to *not* waste your energy on.

And learning when to accept, forgive and let go. As we grow up, grow older, we hopefully are more able to see what we could have done differently to create a better outcome. And maybe next time we encounter a similar situation we will remember what we learned and approach it differently too.

So next we are going to look at acknowledgement, which kind of goes hand in hand with apologising...

Oh no - she's mentioned the A word!!
Apologise? Really??!!

Ok let's stay calm! I know that apologising can be difficult. Oh I really do!

Those words would stick in my throat and I would choke on them! It can be so hard to admit when we're wrong, it's almost as if we're giving in and there is a risk attached to that.

But you know what? Give it a try. It actually doesn't hurt to admit when we're wrong, and it really won't physically harm us to say sorry!

And alongside this, a little acknowledgement goes a very long way to improving a potentially conflicting or difficult situation.

Just so we know what acknowledgement actually looks like, I'm going to take you through a scenario that may or may not resonate for you. But even if it isn't something you have necessarily experienced first hand, hopefully you will get the gist of what it's all about!

Here we go - imagine the following:

You arrive home from work, tired and stressed after a long, hard day. All you want is a nice glass of wine and 10 minutes with your feet up before tackling the pile of jobs you know are waiting for you. But as you step through the front door your partner appears in front of you, and immediately starts telling you all about their day. How the baby wouldn't have her nap, how the older children wouldn't eat their lunch and then drew on the walls, how the dog pooped on the kitchen floor, and how **you** left your wet towel on the bed this morning so it's all damp and smelly and it will have to be changed before anyone can sleep in it, and if you think I'm doing it you've got another think coming...

Whoa there - what a welcome! I can almost see you reeling backwards as this tirade pours out. You hear the kids screeching in the other room, cartoons blaring on the tv, your partner is redfaced and angry, and now the dog is weeing on your shoes in the excitement of seeing you.

So, what is your first thought? Maybe it's why on earth did you bother to come home when you could have stopped and had a drink with your work mates!

What a nightmare! You're tired, fed up, and were so looking forward to that ten minutes of peace and quiet. You're a hard working human being and a hard working human doing your best, and after the challenging day you have had, you deserve it.

So before you can stop yourself, you open your mouth and say, 'for goodness sake, I'm shattered, let me get through the door will you? Stop giving me grief, and can't you control those kids and stop this bl**dy dog from weeing all over me?!'

And there it goes - boom!! Within seconds the equivalent of world war three breaks out. Before you can say another word, you're accused of being an uncaring parent, you're so selfish, it's alright for you, you've been out of the house all day and not stuck here, how dare you speak to me like that, you treat me like a servant... It all pours out, so you get stuck in as well. Neither of you are interested in listening to the other because you just want to vent and say how awful it all is for *you* and how tired *you* are. So it gets worse and finally your partner storms off to the bedroom and slams the door.

So now where does this leave you? Apart from standing in dog wee and listening to what sounds like the kids dismantling the lounge with two small hammers?

Well, fed up and frustrated could be a fair assessment. And probably feeling angry, misunderstood and resentful.

Well, all of those are valid feelings for sure, and they don't feel good, but you can bet your partner is feeling the same.

Ok, so how can this situation be resolved?

Well once again, the first thing to do is take that small step back and look at what happened. Yes, I know that's not going to be easy as you can see the children need attention and the dog wee needs wiping up! So all you can do right now is hang on in there and get on with what needs to be done. If at all possible, try to take a few moments to calm yourself down. Yes, I appreciate this may be hard to do, because you will still be feeling frustrated, upset, criticised, accused, all those things we hate to feel. But just hold on the fact that this situation *is* resolvable, and you have the power! I know that all the shouting and stamping and negative energy probably left you feeling pretty bad and sad and needing more than one glass of that wine.

But the thing is, you can't change anything that was said and done at the time. It's out there, and is now gone. So, it's what you do next that's important and what you need to focus your energy on. Get the kids sorted. Wipe up the wee and let the dog into the garden.

Leave your partner where they are for the moment, and calm yourself down. Remember your breathing - breathing is good - proper breathing, long and slow and deep. Work on letting go of the negative feelings you've been left with as you focus your intention on creating a positive outcome.

Then you need to choose your moment and go and speak to your partner. And right here is the part you are going to change and approach differently. You're not going to bring it all up again or carry on the argument. No, you're just going to tell your partner what happened for you, and why you snapped and ended up shouting.

Now, you may not think you have anything to apologise for because all you did was walk in the door after a hard day and be faced with all that. And you probably have a valid point.

But here's the thing, no situation is ever created by just one person. Have you heard the saying, there are three sides to every story? Your, theirs and the truth? So basically, I think that means we all play our part and it's never all completely one sided.

So, what you are going to do is immensely powerful, it really is. You're going to take control of the situation in a positive way, and start the process of healing and making it better. After all, this is your moment, your time, your day, your life. And if you allow situations to have a negative impact that drag on and on then where is your joy, your moment for a good time, your peaceful heart? Don't allow the situation to steal from you. Summon up your personal power and take positive action.

If your partner hears you acknowledge that you understand what happened and are taking their feelings into consideration, and that you are sorry for your part in it, it will help things immeasurably.

Take a deep breath and have a go at saying something like this:

'I'm really sorry we ended up shouting at each other like that, I was just tired and fed up when I came in. I know you've had a rough day too and I wish I hadn't snapped at you.'

If you can say this with as much honesty and feeling as possible, I can pretty much guarantee that this will take the wind out of your partner's sails. Yes, you might have felt they were unfair in attacking you as soon as you got in the door. But when you break it down, you both had a rough day, and does it really honestly and truly matter who makes the first step to resolving things and making them better? In the great scheme of things, probably not. It's really hard to stay angry and argumentative when someone acknowledges that what they did or said could have been upsetting or hurtful, and it's even harder to stay angry if someone has acknowledged your feelings too. It's almost like sticking a pin in a balloon and letting all the air out, it can be that effective.

You've also given your partner an opportunity to come back with an acknowledgement and or apology of their own. Let's hope that this is the case, but if not, leave them with what you have said and let them think about it. It will be much easier for them to talk calmly about this now that you have offered the acknowledgement to defuse the situation. And we are so much more able to see our own behaviour and feel inclined to take responsibility for our actions when we're calm and not angry with someone else. An acknowledgement from the other person generally releases our anger because we feel understood. Maybe not completely, but it's a great start, which is all good.

* * *

And now here is a potential scenario you may encounter with your teen. It's pretty similar to the previous one in many ways, but you will notice the difference!

You arrive home from work, tired and stressed after a long, frustrating day. All you want is a nice glass of wine and ten minutes with your feet up before tackling the pile of jobs you know are waiting for you. But as you step through the front door your teenage daughter appears in front of you, waving her Ipad under your nose and demanding that you look at this *awesome* pair of *amazing* shoes that are absolutely *perfect* for her prom and you *promised* you'd pay for them, and these are *totally* what she wants and you need to order them *right now*!

Oh my goodness, if only you could get her to be so enthusiastic about cleaning her room or doing her homework!

But as you well know this is exactly what teens and children do. They're not really doing anything wrong, they're excited and they just want your *immediate* attention and expect you to listen and respond straight away.

However, quite clearly this is probably not the moment to get your best attention! You've just walked in the door after a long day at work, but that doesn't register in the teenage world. You're tired, fed up, and looking forward to that ten minutes peace and quiet. You're a hard working human being and a hard working human doing your best, and after a long, hard day you deserve it!

So before you know it, your mouth opens and you say 'For goodness sakes, I'm shattered, let me get through the door will you? And please stop waving that thing in my face!'

And there it goes- BOOM! Within seconds, the equivalent of world war three breaks out!

Before you can say another word, you're accused of being an uncaring parent, you're so selfish, you never let her have anything, why did you even bother to have a daughter because you like *totally* hate her, and now you've ruined her life! And so it goes on, with your daughter shouting and stamping and having a melt down, and out of sheer frustration you end up shouting back, and it gets worse and worse until she storms off to her bedroom in floods of tears.

And where does this leave you?? Feeling angry? Feeling awful? Feeling guilty? Feeling like a failure? Feeling like you wish you could turn the clock back? Feeling like you wish you could emigrate or run away? Feeling desperate? Feeling as if you wish you had a magic wand you could wave to make all these crappy feelings just *stop*?!

Well, I'm sure that we've all experienced something that's not too far away from a situation like this, and it really does feel awful.

But it's okay, don't panic! You can deal with this, and work things out positively, truly you can!

The first thing to do is take that small step back and look at what happened. Don't rush upstairs after your daughter, just take a few moments to calm yourself down, and reassure yourself that you that you haven't actually ruined her life. She will be fine, and this situation *is* resolvable, and fairly easily too.

It's true! I know that all those tears and tantrums and shouting and stamping probably left you feeling pretty bad and sad and needing more than one glass of that wine. But the thing is, you can't change anything that was said and done at the time. It happened, the words were said and the moment is past, now leaving the aftermath to deal with.

So it's what you focus your energy on and do next that's important.

Leave her where she is for the moment and calm yourself down. Forget about feeling guilty, forget about what you both said, find a way to let it go. Remember your breathing - breathing is good - proper breathing, long and slow and deep. Take some time to focus your intention on creating a positive outcome, even though you may feel there isn't one. Trust me - there is!

Then you need to choose your moment, and go and speak to her. Now, this could the hard bit for you to deal with, but you can do it. You're not going to bring it all up again, or carry on the argument. You are the parent, the bigger person, and you are going to let it go.

So, you're just going to tell her what happened for you, and why you snapped at her when you came in. You're human, and humans react in the moment, and that's ok.

Now, you don't need to go into great detail, or extensive apologies or explanations or justifications. After all, she's a teenager, and her attention span probably isn't very long - unless it's all about her! But if she hears you acknowledge that *your* actions contributed to the situation, it will help things immeasurably.

So, making sure you've given her a little time to calm down, go and find her and try saying something like this:

'I'm really sorry we ended up shouting at each other like that, I was just tired and fed up when I came in. I know you're excited about your shoes and I really wish I hadn't snapped at you like that.'

Now, you may notice that you are not saying anything that starts with 'you'.

What you are saying is how *you* feel about what happened. You are giving her an apology (cleverly worded so that whilst you are saying sorry, you are actually highlighting that you both shouted at each other so there is equal responsibility for bad behaviour!).

You are giving her what's called an 'I' message.

You are telling her you felt tired and fed up when you came in after a long day at work, which is reasonable and won't inflame the situation.

You are recognising and acknowledging her excitement over her shoes. And you are quite honestly telling her that you wish you hadn't snapped at her.

If you can say all this and mean it, I can pretty much guarantee that you will take the wind out of her sails. It's really hard to stay angry and argumentative when someone acknowledges that what they did or said to you was out of order. It's almost like sticking a pin in a balloon and letting all the air out, it can be that effective.

You've also given her an opportunity to come back with an apology of her own. She may take it - she may not! And of course there *are* other things to address, like her rudeness, her shouting, her complete over reaction.

But you can talk calmly about this now that you have given her the acknowledgement she needed. Again, we are so much more able to see our own behaviour and feel inclined to take responsibility for our actions when we're calm and not angry with someone else. And an acknowledgement from the other person generally defuses our anger. Maybe not completely, but it's a great start, which is all good.

* * *

So I hope that you can see how powerful acknowledgment can be. Once out in the open, it means the people involved, including you, can move on. Spending time and energy revisiting negative situations, hanging on to resentment, bitterness, frustration and bad feelings only holds us back and hurts ourselves. Why continue to allow the negative energy by rehashing the situation over and over again? It doesn't do anyone any good. Deal with it, release yourself, let go and move forward. You have the power!

Your Golden Rule

Acknowledgement is a wonderfully powerful thing. If you can see how your behaviour might have had a negative effect and you can acknowledge that you might have hurt someone's feelings or made a mistake then you have the power to change things positively for the future. We know you can't go back and change the moment, but you *can* change what happens afterwards. Owning your behaviour, recognising how what you said or did affected someone or something in a negative way and then *saying it out loud* is so powerful. What you are offering is the chance to move on. And this is hugely important when it comes to resolving situations with our children as well. When a situation is done and dusted, move on. Griping and moaning and continually rehashing it will only create negative feelings. It's just not worth it, and it gets in the way of positive progress.

Accept, acknowledge, apologise if you need to, hopefully learn from it, and then move on!

Your moment of Sunshine

Look in the mirror, smile at the person you see there and say 'I love and accept myself exactly as I am'

Now listen, just stop for a moment before you kick off and say 'I can't' or 'I feel silly' or 'I don't believe it so I can't say it!'

You *can* say it. No one else will be there watching, it's just you so there's no need to feel silly. It's only words and they can't hurt you. And they certainly couldn't hurt you as much as the negative criticism you have been giving yourself - but are working on changing now that you are reading this book! And you may not believe the words just yet, but if you say them often enough, you might start to. Remember how we mentioned that children grow up with low self esteem when they hear negative messages, and how we end up feeling about that? Well, try this instead. Try giving that wonderful person you see in the mirror some love, acceptance, acknowledgment and reassurance. Go on, I dare you!

**CHAPTER
FOUR**

RESPONSIBLE PARENTING

We all want to be a 'good' parent don't we? Nobody actually sets out to be a bad parent.

But what if I told you that being a good parent isn't necessarily the best way?

Of course, you don't want to be a bad parent - so what does this mean?

Well, maybe this is the question.

Are you a 'good' parent? Or a 'responsible' parent? And what on earth is the difference?!

Well, let's have a look and find out.

Before we start, let's all agree on one thing. Irrespective of our parenting styles and abilities, we love our children. Full stop. That's it - we just love them.

And we would love to give them the world and keep them safe forever. We hope and pray they will grow up to be successful, satisfied, well adjusted, fulfilled and happy.

So, the million dollar question is how do we make that happen? How can we help them learn to be confident, balanced, responsible individuals, with high self esteem, and the ability to cope with the challenges life presents?

Well, in today's world it seems that parents are often fearful of not giving their children enough. We want to do things for them, and buy them everything we can because we believe this is the best way to show our love for them. Sometimes we end up running round like headless chickens, fetching, carrying, finding things for them, while they sit like little despots issuing their orders! We seem to want to provide a never ending entertainment road show because we hate the thought of them getting bored. We fill their world with toys and gadgets and gizmos to keep them occupied.

And the one word we really seem to struggle with saying is NO!!

'No chocolate unless you eat all your lunch,' we say.

An hour later the whining reaches unbearable levels, and although they didn't finish lunch you hand over the chocolate!

'If you do that again, you won't go the party,' we say.

They do it again - and again - and yet you still take them to the party!

'If you don't go to bed now you won't go to the park tomorrow,' we say.

Bedtime comes and goes, they're still charging around, but you take them to the park the following day!

Listen, I'm not saying it's easy! I've been there, and in the moment we just try to manage as best we can.

But life become more manageable if we provide realistic consequences.

We have to be prepared to follow through on our promises.

And above all, we must mean what we say.

So before you open your mouth and say the first thing that pops out, give yourself a moment to think about it. Consider whether the consequence you are giving them is doable, and whether you will be able to see it through. Because the trouble is, if we keep promising something and then don't keep that promise, then we lose our credibility and authority and they will run rings around us! We need to stand in our personal power!

Maybe you find yourself driving back to school after you've dropped them off with their forgotten swimming kit, home work, lunchbox, mobile phone.

Even though you reminded them a thousand times!

Aren't you kind?

Aren't you wonderful?

And by doing all of this surely you're being a good parent?

You're being caring, kind, loving and helpful.

But hold on just a moment, and think about this. Maybe there is a line where being caring, kind, loving and helpful becomes blurred with just doing *everything for them*. And the result is they don't learn to do anything themselves because they know you will do it instead.

So where does the responsibility lie?

If we always find their shoes how will they ever learn to take responsibility for putting them away and remembering where they are?

If they throw their dinner on the floor and we just keep picking it up and replacing it with more, how will they learn to stop doing that?

If they forget their homework and we rush back to school with it to avoid them getting a detention, will they bother to remember for themselves next time?

Quite simply, this is how it goes.

Real life consists of a series of actions, which result in consequences.

So even as children, if we never have to experience the consequences of our actions, then how do we learn to take responsibility for ourselves as we grow up?

I know we love giving our children gifts. We love seeing their joy and excitement, it gives us such pleasure. So I'm not saying don't give them gifts.

But maybe one of the biggest gifts we can give them is to help them learn how to be responsible for themselves. It costs nothing, but provides everything.

If they learn about boundaries, behaviour, actions and consequences when they are children, then they will be better equipped to take responsibility for themselves as adults.

This world is full of challenges and pressure. And it's my belief our children have a better chance of becoming balanced, well rounded, responsible people if we put boundaries and rules in place to guide them and keep them safe.

The beauty of responsible parenting is that your child is never too young for you to start using this approach.

Our children, toddlers, and even babies actually *want* us to be a responsible parent.

They *need* us to keep them safe with clear, firm boundaries.

They *like* knowing that you mean what you say because this then means that they can trust you.

So this is what I mean by being a responsible parent.

You're not your child's friend, you're their parent.

This means being the person in charge!

So, feel the fear - and say no anyway!

If you create a loving, supportive home with rules and expectations that are consistent and clear then you will build a strong, loving, relationship with your child.

Not as mates, or friends, but as responsible parent and happy child.

So let's have a look at the points below to use as a foundation for this.

- Think about what you want, and set clear boundaries.
- Let your child know what is acceptable and not acceptable.
- Make sure they understand your expectations regarding their behaviour.
- Provide them with consequences for their actions, both positive and negative.
- Help them to understand that they are accountable for their actions.

- Be consistent and stick to what you've said.
- Communicate effectively and clearly - repeat yourself if necessary.

All of this lets our children know where they stand.

All of this lets them know what they can and can't do.

All of this provides them with a solid, safe foundation to build upon.

And most importantly of all, it shows our beautiful, precious children that they can trust us. It allows them to believe what we say and they can then feel safe.

So, we deal with situations as they arise. We provide consequences where necessary. We try to keep it calm, firm and friendly, but we

STICK TO WHAT WE SAY!

I can't tell you how important this is. We are the parent. Our children need our love, care and guidance, and this won't happen if all we do is give in to their every demand, every tantrum, every shout and scream.

They need boundaries, and they need us to be in control.

Now, I'm not talking about enforcing regimental rules, total discipline, physical punishment. When I say firm but friendly this means that you don't have to yell, shout, scream or smack to make your point and be heard.

In fact, think about how you feel when people shout at you. Are you inclined to listen when someone is yelling in your face? How does that feel? Well, I imagine not great, and It's probably just going to make you feel like shouting back, defending yourself, or tuning out and shutting down.

When we start shouting, we are giving away our personal power, and it's all downhill from there. So, remember to stay calm and just speak firmly and assertively. Be clear about what you want, don't be afraid to repeat yourself, and be the responsible parent.

And very importantly, you really have to provide realistic consequences! Going back to the beginning of this chapter I used some examples of meaning what we say and being able to follow through with a firm no. It's pointless to threaten something that you know you are not going to be able to manage! If your child is going to a friends party the following day - there is no way that you are not going to take them to that. So don't use it as a threat because your child will see right through you! If you say something you have to mean it. And I know that can be hard when we are frustrated and fed up and trying to find a way to get them to do what we want. Before we know it we have said something that we don't really mean in the vain hope that they will believe we mean it.

You have to be prepared to back up what you say, so make sure that you are offering a consequence that you know you are going to be able to cope with.

It's the same as making them a promise of something lovely, a treat. If you don't keep that promise you are letting them down. And it's the same with a consequence for their actions, if you don't keep *that* promise too you are still letting them down.

Oh crikey, this must seem like a lot to remember! But it actually isn't. Once you start having faith in yourself as a parent, once you start practicing your new approach you will find your personal power and it all becomes a lot easier.

A great way of helping everyone to understand and remember what is expected of them is to create a list of family rules. Be clear about what you expect from everyone. Keep it positive and happy, not negative and heavy. (And we will look at how to use more positive language a bit later on)

Maybe even have a family meeting and ask for their input, but be careful of getting bogged down and manipulated out of putting rules on that you know you want! You want your child to feel included, listened to, but ultimately you need to make sure that the rules you decide upon are on the list. You don't even have to refer to them as rules. As I said before, the words we use are important. The word rules could have a slightly negative connotation, so maybe talk about a family charter, a contract or guidelines. It's up to you, just make sure you make it work as you want it to.

So, bearing all this in mind, don't be too hard on yourself. You won't always get it right all of the time and some days will be more difficult than others. Try to stay positive and focused on what you are looking to achieve. And if you feel you've got it wrong, try not to worry or let it overwhelm you, just accept you made a mistake and reassure yourself you will try to do it differently next time. Remember how we said life is like a dance? Take two steps forward, one back, skip along and shake your hips, smiling as you go. So focus on the forward steps, accept the backward steps and do a little twirl here and there!

Your Golden Rule

Jam or Marmite?

Who is the responsible person? Who knows best? Well you do!

So, if you want your child to do something, don't ask them, tell them!

Let me give you some examples.

You're out for a walk on a very cold day. Now quite obviously you know your child needs to be wearing their coat, hat, gloves etc. So you say to the child 'Shall we put your coat and hat and gloves on?'

And as is often the case, for no particular reason, the child says no.

Purely out of contrariness, or maybe to test their power and find your limits.

So now you have a potential power struggle brewing over something as simple as you wanting them to be warm. And all because you asked them instead of telling them.

Right from the start just tell them that they need to wear their coat. Don't open up the opportunity for conflict by *asking* them to put it on. You need to **tell** them.

Say something like 'Ooh isn't it cold, come on, lets get your coat on and keep you lovely and warm.' You're not giving them a choice, but nor are you ordering them to do something unreasonable. You are simply being the responsible parent and ensuring that they are warm and won't catch a chill. If they do still say no then it's up to you to insist. Don't back down, don't be afraid of them having a tantrum, or shouting, or showing you up. You are the parent and you know best, so stay calm and focused on getting their coat on. Don't allow them to do anything else until the coat is on. Don't allow yourself to be distracted. Don't lose your focus. Tell them what you need them to do, and follow it through!

Another example might be at bedtime. You say, 'It's time for bed, shall we put your pyjamas on?'

How often does your little one actually say yes to that?! Again, you are opening up a potential challenge just by using the words 'shall we' in a questioning tone of voice, instead of saying 'It's bedtime now, time to get your pyjamas on!'

Of course, it can really help if as you lead up to bedtime you give them a five minute warning, but in a calm and positive way. Say something like, 'I'm really looking forward to reading your bedtime story, so five more minutes and we will go up and brush your teeth ready for bed.' You've given them a clear message, and again it is then up to you to follow through with your promise. You told them you are looking forward to reading them their story, and that they will be brushing their teeth in five minutes time, so they understand what is going on. Then make it happen! Don't be persuaded into 'just another few minutes' or be sidetracked by 'I'm hungry' or other such tactics. You are the parent and you know best, you make the rules and you stick to them.

I want to give you just one more example, and once again it relates to choices.

It's lunchtime and you ask your child what they would like to eat. Now, there doesn't seem to be a lot wrong with that. And for sure, children do like choices, but manageable ones, in bite sized chunks (ooh, lunchtime - see what I did there?!)

So, prevent potential difficulties by just offering them a choice of two things. If it is a sandwich, say something like 'It's time for some lovely lunch now. Would you like marmite or jam in your sandwich?' (And before you protest that those aren't the healthiest options, work with me here! I'm just trying to make a point, and for this purpose, sandwiches with marmite or jam will do!)

You have offered them a choice, and they can decide, but it won't take all day and result in a half hour long discussion about what they want to eat.

Of course, you may have all the time in the world, and want to involve them in the decision making process, and the preparation too. Nothing wrong with that, in fact, time spent making food, working together, creating a learning experience can be good if you have the time. All I am saying is, when necessary and to keep things simple, just offer a limited choice such as jam or marmite!

I used to listen to a friend of mine trying to prepare dinner for her three children. She would smile brightly at them all and say, 'Now what would you like for dinner?'

Oh dear - big mistake! Inevitably, they always wanted something different, and there were arguments and tantrums and tears. I would watch her becoming more and more frustrated and desperate as she tried to manage this and please them all.

So I ask you. How much easier could it have been to just say, 'Right my darlings, we're having yummy fishcakes for dinner tonight. Who would like peas and who would like carrots?' Then the little darlings would know that it was fish cakes, but could feel a little personal power by choosing the peas or carrots, or both! Yes, of course, there may well have been the occasional 'I don't want fish cakes' or even 'I don't like fish cakes' but when she knew that they all loved fish cakes, these were obviously just tactics to upset the apple cart a little. What she needed to do was just stand firm and stick to what she said. At the end of the day it's all a game, and we have to stay one step ahead!

And don't forget about the tone of your voice. So many times I am in a restaurant or supermarket and I hear parents talking to their children, wanting them to sit down or stop running around. And they don't really stand a chance of getting the child to do what they want because they are beaten before they begin by the tone of their voice!

If you sound uncertain, tentative or shaky they will tap into this and respond accordingly. Children are so tuned into us, our moods, our energy, and our lack of confidence in a situation.

If you use a nice strong tone, and are matter of fact, assertive, friendly and calm then they will soon get the message.

A little practice is all you need and you will be positive, powerful parent!

Your moment of Sunshine

I'd like you to remember this little story if you start to doubt yourself, or wonder whether being a 'responsible parent' is the right route to take.

A friend of mine was having problems in her marriage, and eventually she and her husband decided to separate. Obviously this was a difficult time for the whole family and the two children were very unhappy and confused. My friend was devastated, emotionally drained and struggling to cope. She was not only dealing with her own feelings, she was also trying to cope with challenging behaviour from the children at home. They were really pushing the boundaries, refusing to go to bed or do as they were told and she didn't know what to do for the best. It was clear that she allowing all this because she was scared of upsetting them even more by enforcing the rules they used to have and applying any discipline. She was also over-compensating by buying them anything they asked for, but then couldn't understand why they never played with the things she had bought.

But the truth was, the children didn't really want the gifts and toys and games. What they wanted was for their mummy to be the strong, loving and reliable mummy they had always known. Their lives had changed so much, inevitably they were a little lost, confused, sad, worried. And desperately in need of reassurance, continued stability as far as possible, and loving support.

So we put a plan in place for mum to try and get things back on track by reintroducing the discipline that had been missing. The boundaries that told them where they stood. The rules that were necessary for them to feel loved and secure and know that life hadn't changed beyond all recognition and they were still safe.

Just a few days later, the children's behaviour had improved immeasurably. They were going to bed when they were told to. They were listening more and had stopped being rude to her. They also seemed happier and more settled.

Basically, all they wanted was for their mum to show them that she still loved them by keeping their boundaries tight and safe, especially at a very difficult time for them when their daddy was moving out. Children like to know where they stand, and if their boundaries change it confuses and upsets them.

Just keep remembering, you are the adult, you set the boundaries, and you lead the way. By doing this you are reassuring and showing your child that they can trust and rely on you. You can then work on overcoming those feelings of doubt and fear that create confusion, lack of clarity and disempowerment.

Trust your instinct, listen to yourself, stand in your power

MINDFUL LISTENING

A rather wordy title I'm sure you'll agree, but never fear all will be revealed!

So, let's talk about listening.

Well, isn't that just something we all do all of the time?

How can we not? Unless we are hearing impaired we hear what other people are saying and that's that.

Or is it?!

Well, there's hearing, there's selective listening, and then there's mindful listening.

And something we often do in our busy lives is listen without really hearing.

Try and remember the last time you stopped what you were doing, put your phone down and cleared your mind of the million and one things going on in there so you could actually concentrate on listening to someone else. We're often busy, distracted, preoccupied, and don't really focus on actively listening.

So the outcome of this is that we might miss what is really being said, and the person talking to us may not feel valued or heard.

Selective listening is slightly different. This is hearing and interpreting only the parts of a message that seem relevant to you while ignoring or devaluing the rest. Quite often, selective listeners will be deciding upon their response to you before they've heard the full story. It's as if their brain only focuses on the parts of your conversation that they want to hear, and once they have grabbed hold they are hooked into that, and only that. So the whole of the rest of your message becomes lost and irrelevant!

Sometimes when I was talking to my husband or my children, I was convinced that there was an invisible mid air convertor in the room that took the words that came out of my mouth, jumbled them all up, and then fed them into their ears as something completely different. I honestly thought that I was being completely clear about what I was saying, and in fact always prided myself on being a good communicator! But at times I felt may well have been speaking a foreign language.

So upon reflection, I don't think that communication is actually as easy as it appears to be! You would imagine that as human beings we have the ability to communicate very effectively, probably better than any other creature in the world. Look at us! We have a brain that can think thoughts which we transmit to our mouths where we then form words. So all we have to do is open our mouths and say what we are thinking, what we want, what we like, what we need to happen. And as long as the person we are trying to communicate with isn't hearing impaired and speaks the same language then surely they will be able to hear us, understand what we are saying and respond.

Sounds incredibly simple doesn't it?! However, let's remember this about us tricky humans.

We don't always say what we are really thinking.

We don't always say what we really mean.

And we don't always tell the truth!

Humans are complex creatures that can hide behind words, we can say one thing and mean something completely different.

And we often expect people to understand how we are feeling without really telling them.

And we can lie.

Doesn't make us bad, just makes us human!

Now, animals on the other hand seem to communicate very effectively! They learn to live in packs and communities and have hierachies and pecking orders, and they all communicate with each other without words.

I mean, just take a look at dogs. A bit of bum sniffing, lip curling and tail wagging and they have it all sorted. They immediately identify who is top dog, what they need to do to keep top dog happy and then they do it. Animals don't have the ability to hide their feelings or manipulate or lie in the ways that we do. And it seems to work pretty well for them.

So now, I'm not suggesting that we resort to bum sniffing when we meet other humans in the street - although that is an amusing visualisation! But I am just making the point that we don't communicate as effectively as we imagine we do.

Using an I-message

Something that can be really effective when communicating with our children - indeed, with anyone - is to use an I-message.

When you use an I-message, you are providing effective and safe feedback to someone about their behaviour and how it affected you. But you are doing so without a judgement, apportioning blame or putting them down.

An I-message gives the information that

A. describes the behaviour,
B. the feeling the behaviour creates and
C. the effect that the behaviour has.

If you include a description of the behaviour in the I-message this lets the person know what the problem is. This is important because otherwise they won't know what behaviour to change.

An I-message states the behaviour and describes the speaker's feelings (as per A and B). The person giving the message is owning their feelings without being judgemental or aggressive.

And an I-message then offers the opportunity to exchange information, look for a positive way to change the situation, and find a solution.

Example of I-messages

- I feel angry when people call me names.
- I feel hurt when when people ignore me and no one asks what I want to do.
- I feel worried and let down when someone says they're going to do something and then they don't.

You-messages

These are messages that have the word 'you' or 'you're' in them. For example,

- You make me so angry because you forgot to give me a lift home.'

Using You-messages blames the person for the situation and judges them. So the person hearing this may well become defensive or start making excuses, and all of this just makes things worse.

Now, I am not for one minute saying that you don't have the right to feel fed up, angry, let down when someone forgets to pick you up! You may well be thinking yes, it's all their fault and why not blame them because it's their responsibility and they shouldn't forget you! It's not a good way to feel and so it's not easy to stay calm or think about I or You messages! However, it is something that can become easier with practice, and using an I message honestly gets your feelings across in such a better way.

The examples of the I-messages above have been turned into You-message to show this:

- I feel so angry with **you** when **you** call me names.
- I feel hurt when **you** ignore me and don't ask what I want to do.
- I get suspicious when **you're** telling me one thing then I find out **you're** doing another.

So, even though you started by saying 'I' in your message, you then continued with 'you.' So pretty much everything said before the 'you' is generally ignored by the person receiving the message!

As soon as they hear the word 'you', most people are then just waiting for the personal attack they feel is coming.

This can be similar to using the word 'but' in an argument. The general interpretation of this is that you may now ignore and disregard everything that I said prior to the 'but'! For example, 'I agree with you, but ...' is normally followed by listing all the reasons why you do not actually agree with them!

> My son has a t shirt that says:
> 'I'm not arguing with you, I am just explaining why I am right...'
> Love it - so funny, and for so many people so true!

Ok, so an effective I message doesn't contain the word 'you' at all. It's so often construed as a personal attack that it's best to use another word altogether, such as 'people' or 'somebody'. Use of a generic term takes the emphasis off the other person and they are more likely to listen to what you are saying.

Ooh, words and conversations can be such tricky things can't they!?

But luckily there is plenty of information around that offers a whole lot of support, and you could do a whole lot worse that check out my parenting course book from all those years ago. 'From Pram to Primary School' was aimed at parents of small children up to around seven. Then there is a second book entitled 'What can a Parent do?' I guess they are a little dated now - but such a wealth of good information in them.

* * *

Working with the teenagers at Springboard was always an exercise in effective communication!

Using I messages isn't about direct accusation and shaming and blaming, and when describing their behaviour an I message is much less aggressive and inflammatory.

And it was always important to allow the students the opportunity to save face and not look an idiot or a pushover in front of their mates. Once they felt backed into a corner and had no personal power we were much less likely to be able to encourage them to accept the consequences that followed.

One day at Springboard, staff informed me that Michael* (not the students real name) had not managed to complete his work and had been disruptive and rude in the first session of the day. So according to our project rules this meant that he would not be able to go outside for his break, instead he had to stay in and complete an action and feedback form. Always a challenge as obviously the students loved their breaks! However, they also knew the rules, and if they didn't complete the form and miss break then there would be further consequences and so on.

So, I remember catching up with Michael in the hallway as he was heading for the door with his mates. In a quiet and friendly manner I reminded him that he was missing his break, and I would be waiting in room three with his cup of tea and a biscuit. Well, he kicked off, stamping around and shouting that he wasn't coming, he needed to go outside, I couldn't make him…

And he was right. I couldn't make him do anything he didn't want to. But I could encourage him to make a good decision, accept this consequences and then move on. So all I said was, 'I know Michael, it's a pain to have to miss your break - but you can still have your tea and biscuit, and then everything is back on track for the day'.

Well, he was still insistent that he wasn't coming, and headed for the door. But I noticed he was hanging back from his mates a bit and then he went into the toilet. Another member of staff offered to wait and make sure that Michael came to room three, but I said there was no need. Michael knew what was expected of him, it was up to him to make the choice for himself, and I hoped that he would make the right one. He needed a little breathing space and the chance to make his decision. If I had followed him and insisted that he come to room three, and asserted that he wasn't going outside, he had to miss his break and kept on and on - I wouldn't have had a chance! But this way, Michael was able to save face in front of his mates by complaining and kicking off - but he still decided to accept his punishment. He came to room three, drank his tea, completed his form, told me what was bothering him and then was fine for the rest of the day.

So, a combination of things assisted Michael in this situation.

He wasn't shouted at, humiliated or left feeling powerless.

He was treated with respect.

He was given space to work things out for himself after being given the information he needed.

And he still got his tea and biscuit!

* * *

So parents - once again let's not feel bad about our apparent lack of communication skills. We aren't bad people or bad parents. As I said, we are all trying our best to cope with life and all its challenges. It just means we are human, and continuing to learn. Communicating and listening is a skill that can be developed and practised, and you can start anytime you want.

I'd like you to think back to when you were little,

Think of a time when you may have felt excitement, anger, pride, happiness, sadness, grief, jealousy, fear, joy, loneliness, and you wanted to tell someone about it.

Did someone listen to you, show an interest, and encourage you to talk about how you were feeling? If so then lucky you. I would imagine and hope that that felt pretty good

But if this didn't happen for you, what did it feel like? Do you maybe remember feeling upset, disappointed, ignored, let down, maybe even not important enough?

The fact is, we all need to be listened to. We all need to feel acknowledged, validated, and that we are actually worth listening to.

Being listened to makes us feel good.

Our children have a lot to say and want to tell us things, but do we always listen properly? Well I know I didn't. And I don't like that thought, but it's true.

Now, before you say 'Oh no, that's me too, I'm always too busy, I don't listen,' and heap coals of guilt upon your head, remember what I said about being good to yourself?

You've done your best and that has to be enough.

Life isn't easy, we miss stuff, and that has to be okay.

And sometimes the day to day, often repetitive and irritating conversations we have to have with our children can be boring and seem trivial when there is so much else going on we have to cope with. So I guess it's fair to say that sometimes we tune out, it's how we manage daily life and not go bonkers!

But there are times when our children really do need us to listen, and what you can do now is learn how to work on your listening skills for when it really counts, when they need to tell us how they feel.

So like yours, my life was busy. I often felt tired and stressed, and keeping all those balls in the air took concentration, focus and a lot of effort. And I sometimes found it hard to see, hear and acknowledge my children's feelings. But thinking about it now I realise that maybe superwoman was getting in the way. And I wanted my children to be super children! Hearing that they might be upset or struggling with something wasn't good, I just wanted it fixed.

Something else can happen when we are listening to our children, and it took me a long time to recognise and understand it.

When our children are hurt or upset or angry, they can end up pressing buttons that tip us back into uncomfortable times and places in our lives that left us with unresolved issues and may have been hard for us to deal with. Of course, they don't do this deliberately, they don't have a clue about what is going on for us. They are just letting us know how they feel and want us to help them feel better.

So let's see what this might look like.

Your child comes home from school and tells you that they were the last one to be picked for the sports team. Nobody wanted to choose them so they felt inadequate, rejected, embarrassed and sad.

Isn't that a horrible thought? You imagine your little one standing there waiting to be chosen, hoping they will be good enough, and then feeling hurt and disappointed. It's so upsetting to hear, and you probably just want to hug them and make it feel better.

But sometimes what makes it even more challenging is the fact that you remember the same thing happening to you. *Your* experience as a child reminds you that it's a lonely place to be when you are waiting and hoping to be chosen, and nobody does.

So there you are, immersed in your child's pain in more ways than one because your subconscious is reminding you of your feelings of inadequacy, rejection, embarrassment and sadness. Those feelings are uncomfortable and painful, and understandably it might be hard to put those personal feelings to one side and pull ourselves into the present day.

It's not easy to just listen calmly, let them talk it through and help them to deal with it. And our protective nature as a parent makes us want to fix it, make it all better, make sure it doesn't happen again. I mean, come on, who actually wants their children being exposed to situations that might potentially hurt them and leave them with sad feelings? Especially when we know how much that situation can hurt. So the temptation is to just try and make it all better, fix it, give them a great big hug and move on.

Unfortunately though, life isn't full of happiness and sunshine and joy all of the time. Unless we literally wrap our children in cotton wool and keep them hidden from the world they are going to experience things that upset them, hurt them, and make them sad.

So the most wonderful way to help your children to learn, to cope, to process these things is by giving them your time and attention and listening to them. Let them tell you what happened without interrupting. Hear what they are saying without jumping in and trying to fix it for them. Reassure them that it's alright to feel angry, sad, or upset, and it's ok to have these scary, painful feelings. And you are not a bad parent if your child cries. It's a natural and necessary part of life, and if they are able to release in safety with you then they will get over it and can move on.

Be your child's hero. Listen to them.

Your Golden Rule

Focus and comment on the behaviour instead of the person.

If your child has been naughty then instead of saying 'You're a naughty girl/boy and I'm sick of you doing that,' you could try saying something like 'I'm disappointed in that behaviour, I really hope it won't happen again.'

It may sound a little artificial to start with, but with practice you can make it more meaningful and work for you.

Separate the behaviour from the child. Provide a consequence, then let it go and move on. Because we all make mistakes. We all get things wrong and it doesn't make us bad people... we are still worth loving.

Your moment of Sunshine

Your child or teenager may not find it easy to tell you how they feel.

They may be embarrassed or see it as a weakness to talk about their feelings. Boys especially struggle to let their emotions out and can tend to bottle stuff up. But given the chance, most of them *will* talk. We just have to find ways of giving them the safe space and time to do so.

When my beautiful daughter became unwell at the age of fifteen, the next couple of years of our lives revolved around her and our fear of what was going on. It was a hard time for everyone, and we were all just trying to cope and carry on. My husband and I were very focused on caring for our daughter, and our son who was well and thriving had to get on with life and fend for himself at times. I guess that's how it goes sometimes, we were fearful and trying to do the best we could, which as I keep saying just had to be good enough! We were having some family support sessions, and one day our support worker gave us a game to play. Simply called the family game, all you had to do was roll a dice to dictate which category of card you picked from and then answer a question. So nothing particularly complicated or difficult. However, some of the cards were about feelings. Oh no - not the F word!

Well, our son who about 14 at the time was certainly never particularly keen to play when I suggested it, but he never actually refused!

Bless his heart, he did join in, answering the questions and talking about his feelings. One day his card asked him to think about a time he had felt lonely. We all waited while he sat and thought, and then he said 'In this family when Clare was very ill.'

He went on explain how he had felt ignored, left out, and sad at times. But he also said he felt guilty and selfish about telling us this.

Oh those darts in your heart... how they jab and stab and hurt.

Well, I'm sure you can imagine how hard that was for him to share - and then how hard it was for us to hear. Especially for his sister who loved her little brother but could see herself as the cause of his loneliness. And of course she wasn't. My husband and I didn't see what was happening and weren't there for him in the way he needed.

But again, this didn't make us bad people. We were doing out best, and finally Zac was able to tell us how he felt. And we were able to hear him and acknowledge his hurt and pain and make some changes. When I think of my son my heart just sings. I am so proud of the wonderful, kind, funny, clever, caring, beautiful young man that he has become. He brings me nothing but joy and happiness... and all this despite his parents mistakes!

And so the learning curve continued!

ONE STEP AT A TIME

Sometimes life just feels like one big old challenge doesn't it? It can all seem too much and we become tired, fed up, drained and demoralised. It's easy to lose heart altogether when we look at the pile of problems facing us, looking like a mountain waiting to be climbed.

But there is one very important thing to remember about a mountain. Every single one has been climbed and conquered in exactly the same way. Every person started at the bottom and started to climb, taking just one step after the other until they reached the top.

Now that's not to say that there might have been setbacks and problems to solve along the way. But in the end, that mountain was still climbed and conquered by just taking one breath, one step, putting one foot in front of the other and keeping going.

So as I see it, life is like that mountain. Tackle your problems and challenges one at a time. How can you do anything else? I'm sorry to say, you're not superhuman! Of course, what you are is a pretty wonderful, unique and amazing human being doing your best - but superhuman? Not really! So, give yourself a break and stop trying to do everything at once.

Take life one step at a time, one thing at a time, one day at a time, and keep believing in yourself as you go.

Life can be very demanding. How do we prioritise? How do we decide which direction to focus our attention? It can be confusing and overwhelming can't it?

Well, the best thing to do is choose one thing to address and give your full attention. Have a think about what might be causing you the most stress in your home right at this moment.

Just giving you an example to work with:

Maybe it's the fact that your child's bedroom is like a disgusting pig sty, despite all your efforts to make them keep it tidy and clean. Their room is filthy. Their clothes are all over the floor. Dirty washing is mixed up with clean and you can't get them to put it in the washing basket for love nor money. It really gets to you that they keep it in such a state and show no respect for all the nice things you've bought. No amount of nagging, threatening or begging seems to work. Every day, the battle continues. It upsets you. It depresses you. It frustrates the hell out of you! And it is also taking its toll on the whole family because of the arguments and general bad feeling.

Ok - back to Meatloaf - stop right there!

It's time to try something different. Take a new approach and regain your personal power. Think about how awful and energy sapping it feels to have this going on day after day.

Do you want that to continue?

Or would you like to change it?

What would you have to lose if you tried flipping things around and using a positive approach? Nothing seems to be working so far, so let's think about how you can create a positive change.

Choose a time when you are feeling calm and they may be in a receptive mood! Tell your child how you feel but don't make a massive deal about it and go on and on. They know how you feel about their room and you are not going to start this new approach off on a negative note. Remember, you're in your personal power, calm and assertive and trying something different.

Use words like 'I feel disappointed when I see your nice clothes on the floor' or 'I feel really upset when we argue about this' Once again you are using 'I' messages, which is telling them how *you* feel but without verbally attacking them.

What you are going to do is offer them the opportunity to make a responsible and positive choice. Maybe you could say that if they manage to put their dirty washing in the laundry basket and keep their bed room floor clear for a week, you will reward them in some way. Kind of like a star chart - but without the stars!

Now, I can almost hear the cogs in your brain turning as you wonder isn't that just tantamount to plain old bribery?! Well, of course it is! But it's something that you can use as a starting point to underpin and support your new approach to achieving positivity and harmony in your home, so why not?! And of course, the bigger picture is that what you are trying to do is remove the negative attention that they have been receiving up till now, and replace it with a new positive attitude.

Children will try to grab our attention any way they can. They like attention. And if they see that their bad behaviour gets them plenty of it, then they will keep going. Without realising it we often end up paying them huge amounts of attention for their challenging behaviours. We scold, we argue, we shout, we engage in a battle that does nobody any good. And this becomes a habit that takes its toll on us because we can then become too locked into expecting the worst and trying to deal with it, which leaves us feeling exhausted, fed up and demoralised so we aren't inclined to notice anything good.

So, decide on something that you know will tempt them and set this as their goal. Just a word of caution though, make sure it's something that is proportionate to the task. It's really no good going big and offering them twenty quid for a relatively small achievement, because if it works and you make other agreements it'll end up costing you a fortune!

Be smart and offer them something that they would usually manipulate you into giving them anyway!

Of course, the reward is actually not the focus. Well, it may be for them! But it's going to be more about the process, changing the negative situation into a positive, which should result in everyone feeling better.

Now, the success and outcome of this is really going to be down to you!

Over the week, you will need to stay as calm, positive and assertive as you can. If they don't appear to be engaging with the plan try not mention it or make negative comments.

Yes, I know it won't be easy, but keep focused on what you're trying to achieve. Remember how awful you felt when you were shouting and being angry with your child. How your energy was drained by the constant battle. Remind yourself that you are taking control of this situation in a positive way and creating change for the better.

Just offer a gentle reminder of what they have to gain if they manage to keep their part of the agreement instead of pointing out that they haven't done it, and then change the subject. Don't allow them to keep pressing your buttons or wind you up. Take back your personal power!

If they choose not to do it, then they won't get the reward, it's as simple as that. But if you have handled this right, stayed positive, friendly and calm, I will be surprised if you don't achieve what you have set out to do.

So hopefully you will see positive results. Your child will feel good about the fact that they have been rewarded for doing something, and you have stopped screaming at them! You will feel better because you took control of a situation and made a positive change. So now you will hopefully feel empowered to approach another challenge and solve it. Remember the mountain? One breath at a time, one step at a time, and just keep putting one foot in front of the other.

* * *

I'd love to share a story with you that really helped me to understand the concept of positive attention over negative reaction.

My children were both great sleepers, usually in bed soon after seven o'clock and sleeping twelve hours through the night.

But one morning Clare came into my room at around six o'clock, complaining that Zac had been into her room and woken her up. My husband and I spoke to Zac, told him this was naughty and he had to stay in bed until it was time to get up. He was four, old enough to understand, and we thought that would be the end of it. However, over the next few days the situation continued with Zac waking Clare up earlier and earlier every morning. I couldn't work out what was going on, and we spoke to Zac again, telling him what he was doing was naughty and we would have to punish him if he continued. But he didn't stop. So my husband and I decided to tell Zac that if he woke Clare the next morning, he would get a smacked bottom.

Oh Lord, I am actually cringing as I read that! I can't believe that I thought that smacking our children was acceptable. But things were different in those days, and smacking was commonplace and accepted as a form of discipline. So, we were confident that this would deter him, and the situation would be resolved. Until the following morning when once again Zac went into Clare's room and woke her up. We were amazed. Why was he doing this? We had clearly told him he would get a smack if he woke his sister again. So, we had to follow through with our threat, and Zac received his smacked bottom. And he was told that if he did it again, next time he would have two smacks.

Please, I feel bad enough as it is! And yes, you've guessed what happened. Zac did the same the next morning, and then the next.

Quite why on earth my husband and I couldn't see any other way of resolving this I have absolutely no idea. We were two fairly intelligent people but it's as if we were blinkered and became hooked into a situation that we couldn't stop, and were powerless to change. So nothing changed because we didn't know how.

But luckily help was at hand, and we found the support we so desperately need from a parenting course that we had recently signed up for. I do believe that everything happens for a reason and at the right moment, and this was incredibly fortunate timing.

Each week we had the opportunity to discuss our progress and any challenges we were experiencing, and so I shared our problem with the group. I can honestly still recall the look of horror on the face of the lady next to me when I admitted we were up to seven smacks and my husband and I were arguing about whose turn it was to smack our son because neither of us wanted to. I can feel the horror in my soul as I write this, and I remember the feelings of helplessness and frustration. It just goes to show how easily you can become overwhelmed, lose your ability to think clearly, and feel powerless to stop making bad decisions.

But with the help of the facilitator and the group, we were able to find a better course of action. And my gratitude and relief were immeasurable!

What we decided to do was use a star chart to change Zac's behaviour. I'm sure you have heard of them, and basically this was just a big piece of paper with the days of the week and spaces to stick stars. The idea was that every morning he *didn't* wake his sister Zac would be praised positively and stick a star on his chart. And when he got seven stars he would win a small prize. Nothing massive, just an acknowledgement of his achievement. We didn't go overboard with the praise, just a smile and a hug and a comment, and then help him to choose and stick his star on.

Instead of using negative language, threatening and promising punishments, we switched it around and were able to celebrate his better behaviour in a positive way. We were all a whole lot happier, and Clare was getting her full nights sleep again!

However, nothing is all plain sailing, and despite the great progress it seemed we weren't completely done with the early mornings. Four days in we were feeling pretty good, maybe we had cracked this!

And then Zac woke his sister up early again.

What was going on? Was this the end of our wonderful plan? Was it all going backwards? Had we failed?

Well no it wasn't any of those things. Zac had just decided to test us out and see if we meant what we said. As most children will do!

So, there was my gorgeous little boy standing by his star chart waiting to find out what was going to happen.

Would he be scolded?

Would he get a smack?

Would he get a star anyway?

And here it was! My moment of positive, powerful parenting. I looked down at him and said in a disappointed tone of voice 'Oh dear Zachary, what a shame you woke Clare up, you won't get a star today. Never mind, maybe you'll get one tomorrow.'

I clearly remember the look on Zac's face as I saw the realisation sinking in. He wasn't getting a smack. He wasn't hearing his mummy shouting and scolding. He just wasn't getting his star. And stars meant prizes! His bottom lip wobbled slightly. But I was firm, friendly and positive. Responsible mummy in all her glory and it was wonderful! I felt powerful, calm, and totally in control.

We went down stairs to have breakfast and Zac never woke Clare early again. He stuck all his stars on his chart, got his little prize, and we moved on.

But I had learned a great lesson, and I never forgot it. I realised that the impact of that positive approach was massive. It was a real turning point for me to understand how to provide boundaries and consequences without screaming, shouting or smacking.

Of course, I'm not suggesting that every situation will be resolved with a handful of stars to stick on a star chart! But I really hope that you can see how effective this alternative approach can be. Rewarding children for bad behaviour with lots of attention just doesn't work, and doesn't feel good either. Ignore as much of the bad as possible and create something positive. You will see the results, I promise.

However, a final thought about this wondrous event. Reading over what I have just written I realise that I still missed something in this glorious moment of positive parenting. I forgot to acknowledge with Clare that she was the child behaving beautifully in the face of all this. She was being woken up each morning. She was tired and fed up with it. But all she saw was the attention that Zac was receiving. And she didn't get a star chart, or a prize.

I missed that one, and I don't like the feeling in my chest when I think about it. But I can't change it and it won't do any good for me to dwell on it.

All I can do is share this feeling with you, and hope that it creates an opportunity for you to do something different and benefit from it.

This also makes me think of the time Zac came home from school with four stickers on his certificate which he had received for good behaviour and achievement. I thought he would be happy with this and praised him for his achievement. But he appeared indifferent and when I asked what was the matter he just said that he had only received two certificates that year. I tried to say that this was a good achievement, but Zac said there was a boy in the class who already had five. And this was the same child who had punched Zac in the face a few weeks before, knocking his glasses off and making him scream in pain. The child clearly had behavioural issues and was always in trouble, and Zac just couldn't understand how someone could be so badly behaved but still get so many stickers.

It's a tricky one isn't it? Of course, the schools want to motivate and praise, and find ways of recognising effort and achievement. But it seemed to Zac that you could hit someone and behave badly a lot of the time, but still receive stickers for the moments of good behaviour that occasionally occurred. Zac behaved himself all the time, was a model pupil, but didn't get half the stickers this other boy did. At the age of 5 my son had worked out that the system was somewhat flawed and was already feeling disappointed and demoralised. The children who shouted the loudest and behaved the worst STILL got the most attention.

This was a difficult one to deal with and try to explain. Quite clearly it appeared to Zac that there were greater rewards for badly behaved children. I tried to explain that different children needed different support, and bolster Zac up by telling him we were proud of him and his good behaviour. But at the age of five life isn't meant to be that complicated, and I'm not sure he believed me.

Thinking back, that was actually when Zac's behaviour at school took a bit of a downward slide. Hardly surprising when you think about it.

And you know what? I've only just made the connection.

Wow… remembering these things and writing this book really is one heck of a journey!

So maybe the system just needs some tweaks and adjustments in larger environments such as schools, but I still stand by my belief that positive attention and praise is better than negative attention for bad behaviour.

* * *

Your moment of Sunshine

Just remember this. Our society has all these standards and expectations. It has categories it likes us to fit into. It applies labels and judgements and wants us to fit neatly in place and be 'normal.'

But the truth is, we are individuals, unique souls, no two of us are the same. Maybe that sounds a bit scary to some people. But honestly, how can we compare ourselves to another person? Surely that's impossible! Because we are all different, and it's alright to be different. In fact, it's more than alright. It's wonderful to be different. Try to relax and enjoy, embrace your differences.

Don't waste your time comparing yourself to anyone else. Really, why would you? Celebrate the unique, beautiful you and keep taking those steps towards greater acceptance, recognition and love for yourself.

And I'm going to risk mentioning
the F word... Forgiveness

Try to forgive yourself - and forgive others.

I know that releasing and letting go of pain, hurt, resentment, anger is not easy. And why should we? If someone has wronged us, hurt us, let us down, taken something from us we have a right to feel bad don't we?

Of course we do!

But the thing is - what good does it do us to keep revisiting what has happened? Don't **allow** someone or something to take our happiness from us. Accept it has been said. Put it away, let it go, don't keep going over and over it.

Look at it this way. Why allow something to affect us negatively and steal our time?

Letting go can set us free and be wonderfully empowering.

This is our life. This is our time. This is our moment. This is our joy. Make it count.

Your Golden Rule

Keep looking for that Sunshine 4 your Soul.

Keep releasing your personal power and creating positivity and harmony, in this moment, and then the next. Because that is all there really is. You know that the past is exactly that, it's past. It's gone and we can't change what happened. The future is ahead of us. The next hour, the next day, the next week, month, year. And as we really never know what is around the next corner, this moment is what we have. If we focus on worrying about the future we may well miss the most important bit, which is right now. So grab the moment, appreciate it, be grateful for it, and live your beautiful life one breath, one step, one day at a time.

CHAPTER SEVEN

NICE WORDS PLEASE

Because I believe that the words we use are hugely important. The messages we receive have a deep and long lasting effect on how we feel about ourselves and how we end up behaving.

If we hear negative things about ourselves then we will believe them and live up to them.

It's a fact that children who grow up with criticism and negativity will have lower self esteem.

So many of the teens I've worked with were told they were lazy, stupid, disruptive, useless, trouble makers... negative words and labels that they ended up believing and living up to.

And although we know it's not always that easy it really is so important to try and stay as calm as possible and avoid these negative words. Try to avoid name calling and shouting and yelling. And if we want them to do something, try asking instead of telling them, or barking an order and expecting an immediate response.

How do you feel at work, or indeed, in any environment, when someone orders you to do something, or speaks rudely or shouts at you instead of asking you nicely? Do you feel inclined to do what they are telling you to do? Probably not!

Now, this may seem a bit of a turn around to what I talked about earlier. I advised parents to not *ask* their little one to put their coat on, or get into their pyjamas, but to tell them. Firmly, but nicely and assertively.

But I'm now talking about older children and teens. We have to be smart and adopt a different approach! Read back over the Mindful Listening chapter, it might help.

So what we are going to do is start by looking from a child's perspective.

When we were little babies we were cute, and cuddly and sweet and gorgeous. We were kissed, and sung to, and read to, and played with, and hugged and loved and told over and over again how beautiful and good and clever and lovely we were.

So the words we heard were loving, encouraging and reassuring.

Then we grew into toddlers. Still cute, cuddly and sweet, still being told we were gorgeous, still being encouraged. But now our personalities were developing, we were becoming a little more independant, wanting to explore. We started to experiment, find out how things worked, and our routines expanded beyond just being held and fed and going to sleep. There was a whole world out there, wonderful new sensations, new toys to play with, new people to meet. And we had to rely on our mum or dad or whoever was in charge to keep us safe while we explored.

So this meant that we needed some nice firm boundaries! We needed to know what was right and what was wrong, and how far we could go.

And at the same time we were also learning how to push our parents buttons, how to be defiant, how to manipulate situations and get what we wanted! And this only increased and magnified as we grew older.

And then before you know it your sweet little darling becomes a teenager!

Oh, that word! Shades of Harry Enfield and Kevin and Perry – in some respects, so true to life and totally hilarious. That scene where on the stroke of midnight Kevin turns thirteen and transforms into a teenager is utterly inspired. Everything changes and we find ourselves laughing at the hair, the new voice, the hanging arms, the rudeness to his parents.

But hey, I guess it's not quite so funny when you find yourself living with one,or two, or three...!

So for a parent, it's sometimes not so easy to stay in that happy, positive, loving space. We still love our children, of course, we do. But we can often become frustrated and demoralised and negative. And that is when we can lose our personal power.

Now, I'm going to make a bold statement here and say that I would challenge anyone to say that they love and adore and enjoy their children everysecond of every minute of every day! Look, of course we love them. Of course we adore them. But let's be completely honest. Children can be noisy, messy, silly, annoying, repetitive and even a little tiresome! I don't think that I am being unkind, I think I'm just being honest!

But here's something that we may not have considered. Quite possibly we get on their nerves as well!

Always telling them we know best, telling them what to do, making decisions for them and about them, putting restrictions in place, reminding them that they don't know everything, telling them to put this away, clear that up. They probably get fed up with it all and sometimes wish we would just be quiet!

So how do we create a more harmonious existence?

Well, maybe we need to relax a little at times.

Now, I don't mean we drop the ball, relax the boundaries and start letting them get away with stuff! Absolutely not, they need us to stay firm, consistent, strong and assertive. But maybe it's alright to let them have an opinion, or disagree with you, or even have the last word at times.

That dreaded last word! It can really create a problem. We all want to have it don't we?! Especially most of the teens I've worked with!

But as long as they understand that at the end of the day you are letting them know what is required, there are actions and consequences, and that you're in charge, it's not the end of the world if they kick off and perform a little, maybe stamp around, threaten defiance and slam the door as they storm off. At least they will have felt they got to make their point and be heard, even if you don't agree with what they are saying! And they will then have an opportunity to calm down. All I am saying is, don't make every argument or disagreement a battle that you have to win at all costs. Yes, you may feel they are speaking disrespectfully, they may be shouting, they may be talking over you. But just remember, *you* are the parent, and at the end of the day you make the final decisions. So make a judgement call as to whether it really matters that much if they sounded off a little. Some people would say pick your battles - but if you use the word battles that implies a fight and a war. No, I would say just choose where and how to use your energy, and remember that positive words create positive energy and outcomes.

Really importantly, don't talk about things you don't want them to hear or know about when they are around. And don't talk about them either!

Because even though it doesn't appear that they are, our children watch, listen to and are aware of everything we do. Oh, please don't be fooled by the fact that they are constantly on their phone, or seem absorbed in a tv programme, or a game. You think from their non committal, distracted answers to a question, or the fact that you have to repeat yourself when addressing them that they aren't listening. They appear not to notice what is going on around them, but believe me, they are quietly soaking everything up and absorbing it. Filing it away for future reference. Remembering every word!

So, if you want to discuss something that you really don't want them to hear then make sure they aren't present. And if you need to talk about them, make sure they aren't around and really can't hear you. Think about how uncomfortable it would be if your work colleagues were discussing you or your behaviour right there in front of you. How would that feel? Pretty awful I can tell you! So make sure they don't hear you talking about them.

I'd also like to mention something that appears more and more frequently nowadays - and that's the word 'banter'.

The Oxford English Dictionary defines banter as:

"The playful and friendly exchange of teasing remarks - or exchanging remarks in a good humoured teasing way"

So what is wrong with a bit of banter?

Well, nothing really, if indeed what is being said is good humoured, teasing, playful and friendly. Banter is everywhere. And the word is used endlessly to sum up all kinds of interchanges and teasing. But unfortunately, it has now become a permissible way to verbally abuse someone, be unkind, and is sometimes little better than bullying. Think about this. I might say to you, 'Oh my God you're such an ugly fat minger.' Which is horrible! Is that banter? No, I don't think so - I see that as just being unnecessarily unkind and calling someone names. But by today's standards, apparently it's alright as long as I give it the label of 'banter.'

I won't go into this too deeply, but I'm just using this word as an example of what is going on today, and how we often feel it is ok to be verbally abusive to someone else in the name of amusement and entertainment.

Words hurt. And I think that it is up to us all to try and be aware of the words we use and how they may affect someone else.

Yes, be funny, humour and laughter is good - but something that may seem funny to you often isn't to someone else.

Think about the words you have heard used about you and how they may have hurt or niggled or upset you.

And just try to be kind. Banter is fine - when it truly is light hearted and humorous and playful. Don't look for laughs at another person's expense. Don't become a banter bully.

So, following the theme of nice words and how to make changes, let's look at how to create a positive start to the day. And whilst this is based on younger children in the examples, exactly the same thing applies to our older children and teens. If the first words they hear are critical or negative then they will more than likely respond in the same way. So when you are reading this section just make appropriate changes and apply it to your older children.

Ok, so you know the feeling. The kids have had you up half the night, won't stay in their own beds, running around, and consequently had you running around after them. Exhausting, draining and demoralizing, and now you have another morning to face when you feel knackered before you start and cross with yourself as well as them because you feel like a failure.

So before you know it, your day gets off to a bad start because you are already feeling negative, and this communicates itself to the kids.

Parenting never stops does it?! And I'm sure that most of us wake up and try to begin every day with good intentions, see it as a new start, face it with a more positive outlook. But are then are often frustrated and disappointed when we find ourselves back in the same place! Shouting, cross, upset, and late!

It's so tricky to manage everything that needs to be done, let alone cope with attention seeking and seemingly obstructive children. Especially when you may be on your own, going through emotional turmoil because of your own stuff, feeling low before you have even started the day.

So, I'm going to show you how to take some tiny steps towards improving your start to the day, and hopefully making some positive changes.

I recently spent some time with a family who were really struggling. Mum had three children, and was coping on her own after her relationship had recently ended.

Each day was a struggle and mum found herself stuck in a seemingly never ending downward spiral when it came to managing the children. It started with getting them ready for school and nursery in the morning, there never seemed to be enough time to do everything that needed doing.

The oldest child would try to get his mums attention in any way he could. I could see him watching her, and as she was trying to feed the baby and get the three year old sorted he would announce that he had lost his trousers, or couldn't find his socks, or demand to know where his Ipad charger was, or state that he didn't like the cereal for breakfast and wanted something different. Mum was busy, under pressure to get everyone ready, so sometimes it was all too much and she would end up shouting at him. Which of course just made her feel worse but she didn't know what else to do. Why couldn't he find his socks? Why wouldn't he just eat his cereal? Why was he asking about his Ipad charger when she had clearly told him that he didn't have time to play it at that moment?

But children will get our attention however they can, and often when they can see you're under pressure, going to be late and rushing around, their behaviour becomes worse. They are trying to attract your attention - because any attention is better than no attention! This might sound odd, because who actually wants someone shouting at them or being cross? But it's what they do. And this little boy was just making sure he got mums attention by pressing her buttons and being 'annoying'. So this then resulted in her giving him attention in a negative way, but it was all she knew how to do. Just as I was when Zac was waking Clare up!

So now, how to make some changes to this pattern of behaviours? Well, you may recall we covered some pointers towards this earlier in the book, but maybe it would be a good idea to remind ourselves of them again here.

First thing to do is that switcheroo. Replace the negative with positive.

It's so important to reinforce positives, I can't emphasise this enough!

It's not always easy to change old habits, but taking little steps is the way forward. It's so easy to get hooked in, and while I know it's much easier said than done it really is the best thing to ignore the irritating behaviours that our children display to press our buttons and get our attention any way they can. It's like going fishing. they cast out the bait, we grab the hook and then they reel us in!

So much of this is about finding and regaining your positive power, which you may well have ended up giving away because you are tired, stressed, snowed under and just simply sick of it all.

So look at making some changes.

In the case of this family mum started trying to begin the day by saying something positive. I advised her to stop what she was doing, make sure she was looking directly at him and that he was listening. Then she would work on finding something positive to say, along with a smile.

If the first words he hears you say when he wakes up (or wakes you up!) are negative or critical ones, then that will set the tone for the day. Just imagine how you would feel, or maybe have felt when the first words you hear when you wake up are someone sounding cross with you. And if you see a frowning face instead of a smile. It's not a nice feeling, so really try hard with this, because it's very important.

Of course, it doesn't mean that your child will then magically behave perfectly, usually nothing is quite that easily fixed - but you might well get the day off to a better start which can only help.

Also very importantly, remember to ask them to do things in a positive way. For example, instead of saying 'For goodness sake, where are your clothes, I asked you to get dressed!' Try to say something like 'It would really help mummy a lot if you would get dressed now - your clothes are on the sofa/in the bedroom/etc'.

And if you can't remember where the clothes are, ask him to be very clever and find them! Asking him this way will generally get a better response than if you are shouting or ordering. Let him take responsibility, suggest where to look, and if he finds them then offer lots of praise.

Another thing to try to remember is to give him specific instructions, make sure he's listening, and try to keep calm. We often think we have said something clearly, and are then frustrated when the child doesn't do what we have asked. But maybe they just weren't listening or engaged at that moment. Check that they have heard you, repeat yourself if necessary, ask them if they understand.

And it's ok to ask him to help you, he will actually like that. Find something he can do to help, even just a little thing, so that you can say, 'I'm so pleased you did that, it's so helpful for mummy, thank you'

Now I know all this sounds easier said than done especially with three children to manage! But these little things will help to make things calmer and easier as time goes on. Take everything just one step at a time ok? And don't worry if you have a bad morning, there's always a new day coming and a chance to start again, so don't focus on the negative, what you feel didn't do, what you think got wrong, what you feel could have done better. Beating yourself up and telling yourself you've failed - again - will do you no good at all. In fact, remember what we said before, it's a complete waste of your time and energy. Learn from what happened, and tell yourself you will try to do it differently next time. You're human - we make mistakes, we get it wrong sometimes - end of!

And then at the end of the day - Positive bedtime routines

After a long busy day, here comes bedtime again. We are often much brighter in the morning, more able to cope. When we are tired and worn out by the days events things can feel so much harder to deal with.

So, if bed time has been something of a battle in your house - change the energy! Do something different. Try to get into a positive frame of mind, as you start preparing for the bedtime routine. Focus on your objective, which is getting your child/children to bed!

Make bath time as much fun as possible, and then try and spend a little time just winding down with them before bed. Let them tell you things, listen to them, and then calm things down.

Try reading a story, use oils/sprays, give them a head rub, sing a song together, give them a foot rub, anything to calm them a bit and get them ready for sleep. Try not to get hooked into feeling cross or upset about water on the floor after bath, wet towels left lying around, mess and clothes all over the place. Bedtime isn't the time to start clearing up (although I appreciate the wet towels have to be picked up or they will pong!) so leave everything and concentrate on getting the routine in place.

If one of the children says they don't want to listen to the story, try not to make a big thing of it, just say something like 'oh that's a shame - well I'm going to read it to your sister/brother anyway'. They might come to listen and join in, or they might not. Try not to get hooked in to anything that they do or say at this point, don't argue with them about where their ipad charger is, or whether you said they could go skydiving out the window. They may well try to distract you and get your negative attention again, don't let it happen! Stay focused on what you are trying to achieve. Stay calm. Read the story.

And the thing to remember is, this might not all work straight away. You sometimes have to try things over and over again to get them in place, same as you have to keep repeating yourself sometimes. It's what I call the broken record response. They are asking 'why can't I do that?' and they ask again and again, and they have a million reasons why they should be allowed to, and all their friends do it.

So in the face of this you stay calm, you keep focused, and when necessary you just repeat yourself. Don't give in, don't get hooked in, your response continues to be the same, but delivered calmly and without shouting.

Your moment of Sunshine

Something else that is important is authentic praise. Kids are clever, they know when we aren't really paying attention, or are being inauthentic.

Your five year old brings you a painting they just finished. You take a quick look - after all, you're pretty busy, dinner to cook, washing to do, and you say 'Oh darling, isn't that wonderful, you're so clever!'

Sounds great doesn't it? So, what's wrong with that, I hear you ask?

Well, nothing of course. You didn't ignore her, you acknowledged her painting, your were enthusiastic.

But the painting was just one big yellow splodge. Definitely not her best effort and you know it. And she knows it too! You've seen her paint dogs and cats and trees and cars. And this is literally a yellow splodge.

Now, there is nothing wrong with splodges! Maybe she was in the mood for painting a splodge instead of a cat, or a dog or a tree or a car. But what I am trying to say is, why not let her know that you have actually looked at her painting and really seen it by saying something positive and relevant to the splodge?

It's yellow. There's a lot of yellow. So maybe you could say something like 'I love how you have used so much yellow. It's the colour of sunshine and makes me feel happy.'

You're letting her know you feel happy and positive about her lovely yellow splodge, but you haven't pretended it's a work of art, and she will know and appreciate this. Children love us to notice things, they love positive feedback, and they love us to be authentic.

And find something to give authentic praise to your teenager about This may be harder work, but there will always be something and it's important that they hear positive praise and feel we have noticed them. Even if it's something as trivial as putting their cup in the sink or dishwasher. Hanging their coat up. Not tramping mud all through the house. Anything positive that you can find and mention and say something like 'Thanks for putting your cup in the sink/hanging your coat up/remembering to take your shoes off… And then don't spoil it by saying 'Now get upstairs and clean that pigsty of a room out!!!'

Focus on the positive moment. And smile while you do so!

Don't worry, this is all going to so much easier than it sounds - you've got this!

Your Golden Rule

Remember, nice words equal positive encouragement

When I started my first term at Vyners Grammer School I was nervous, apprehensive, scared. But also excited and full of anticipation. The school seemed enormous. I couldn't imagine how I would ever find my way around. I was always very aware of looking foolish, so worried about people seeing my vulnerability, or my 'lack', possibly thinking I was stupid. So on my first day in the maths class, I was desperate to make a good impression. Our teacher was a small German lady who was for some reason wearing a white scientists coat. Anyway, after greeting us all, she set us a task. I can't remember what it was, but I do know it was something that I felt confident I could achieve, which pleased me greatly. Here was my opportunity to shine! She asked us to put our hands up when we had finished and I diligently set to work. Upon completion, I looked up, and realised that I was the first to finish! Quite frankly this was pretty amazing, as maths had never been my strongest subject! So with great delight and enthusiasm I put my hand up. The teacher looked pleased, and I felt a warm glow inside at what I felt sure would be her approval and praise.

She walked over to my desk and picked up my book. I waited for the praise, the congratulations - but instead of marking it she dropped it back onto my desk and said, 'Stupid girl, you have written it in pencil. I am not marking that.'

Well, she may just as well have slapped me. I was bemused, furious, humiliated… and what was wrong with writing in pencil? I always did in primary school, so I questioned what had I done wrong? She basically ignored me and moved onto the next person with their hand up, and I felt terrible. Apparently she had told us to use pen, but I hadn't heard her.

Now, this may sound trivial. It may sound as if it *was* my fault, as she had told us to use pen. So I had to take responsibility for not listening. But on that first day when there was so much going on could she not have handled that a little differently? And being called a stupid girl in front of the class felt really crappy.

Quite honestly, that demoralised me so much that I didn't want to bother to try again. I felt foolish, humiliated, exposed, disappointed. I had so wanted to make a good impression, I had worked hard only to be treated like an idiot. So I wasn't going to try again. I wasn't going to risk getting it wrong again, being embarrassed, feeling silly.

So, I guess my point is this. I used pencil instead of pen, fact. However, if the teacher had handled that a little differently, used more positive encouragement instead of just refusing to mark my work and telling me I was stupid, I may not have been so demoralised and stubbornly defiant in my approach to much of the rest of my school life!

Children are sensitive souls. They need to hear positive words, encouragement, praise. If children hear negativity, criticism, sarcasm, derogatory comments, they will grow up with low self esteem.

Yes And No

Such little words! Only three letters in yes, and two in no. But they are probably the most important words we use. Telling our children 'yes' or 'no' really shouldn't be that difficult. But nowadays it seems to be something of a challenge, and 'no' really does seem to be the hardest word.

Ok, so remember that as a parent you are the responsible adult in the relationship, and as such you're the one who has to make the decisions. Your child will inevitably question those decisions and might push the boundaries to the limit to test whether you mean what you say and can be trusted to stay consistent.

Children need us to keep them safe, by showing them the way, by being strong and reliable, and by not being afraid to say **no**. When they grow up and move out, go to work, their world is not going to be filled with people falling over themselves to run round after them, tidy up after them, let them off the hook if they're late or rude or behave badly, or say *yes* to everything they want! This just isn't going to happen, and we are not preparing them properly for real life if we don't keep the boundaries and guide them in the right direction.

So this is where more of this 'responsible parenting' comes in! Have the courage to believe that you know best. Have the courage to say no. If you provide boundaries and say '*no*' at times now, then they will be better equipped to face their futures and take responsibility for themselves out there.

And despite what seems to be a popular belief, saying no is not being unkind! We need to provide them with the understanding that they can't have what they want all the time, or say or do whatever they want.

Life will not always provide us with exactly what we want when we want it. There will be school, rules, lessons, jobs. We can't just do as we please, and if as children we are never told no, it sets up an expectation that will be sadly difficult to cope with when we come up against a world that doesn't want to give us everything we want!

So, be brave, learn when to say no as well as yes. And remember, it's all in how you say it!

You might find this next piece helpful when it comes to staying firm, but in a positively powerful way. Being assertive is a way of doing this and I can remember how amazing it felt the first time I really came to understand and appreciate the power of assertiveness. And with practice it got easier and I became better and better at it.

So, I will share my first experience - maybe it will resonate for you - maybe not!

When my children were young, I spent a lot of time with my sister in law. She was a strong, capable woman and we had a good relationship. We lived in the same village, and she worked hard to provide for her two boys. We helped each other out with baby sitting, listened to each others moans about husbands etc, and sank many a bottle of wine together! But over a period of time I began to feel a little resentful of the amount of time she was asking me to mind her children. I found it hard to say no, and I was becoming increasingly frustrated and negative. I loved my nephews, but it seemed I was having them more and more, it felt like a chore which didn't feel good.

Luckily, I seemed to find some help at just the right moment.

Wow, looking back I can see that how at relevant times in my life I seemed to be in the right place at the right time to access the help I needed to work out how to cope and make changes if necessary. Sometimes life just provides you with what you need. Maybe just like this book!

I had signed up for an Introduction to Counselling course, as I wanted to be a volunteer at a youth counselling and advice service called 'Time to Talk'.

One evening the course content was all around assertive behaviour, and looking at the difference between behaving passively, aggressively or assertively. I was fascinated, and soon started to understand that I had mainly fallen into the aggressive category throughout my life! Passive certainly didn't seem to describe me, and although I would have liked to imagine I was an assertive person, I'm not convinced that I particularly was.

Now, before I carry on, all this may well sound a bit psychobabble and confusing, so at the end of this section you will find some definitions and explanations about these different behaviour types that I hope will help make it all clearer.

A couple of days after my counselling course, my sister in law called me and asked me if I would look after the boys the next day. And usually this would have resulted in me feeling under pressure, and unable to say no. This wasn't necessarily because she was being pushy or forceful, it was because I didn't feel confident or comfortable in saying no.

What if she got upset with me?

What if she didn't like me anymore?

What if she thought I was just being selfish?

All these thoughts and feelings would arise, and even if I felt like saying no it never really came out very assertively. And she would just say something like 'Oh please, I'm really stuck, haven't got anyone else to have them,' and I would cave in like a house of cards in a draft because I felt I couldn't let her down.

But what I didn't realise was that I was letting *myself* down by not considering my needs, and this in turn had an effect on my children. Because most times I would come off the phone angry and resentful and fed up with myself for not saying no properly. I was being put upon, and not feeling any value or consideration as a person in my own right, but was unable to see that all of this was down to me! My sister in law was just doing what she had always done, and she didn't know that I felt this way because I never told her. And I never said no. So, now I became queen martyr, moaning to my husband when he came in about having to look after *his* nephews for *his* sister again. Poor bloke, he had been at work all day and would come home to my miserable face and moaning voice - as if it was his fault! I just wasn't able to see my responsibility in the way I was responding and behaving, and that I could change things if I really wanted to.

And at my counselling course, this is what I learnt. I always had a choice whether to say yes, or no. It didn't feel like it because of the pressure I felt, but most of that came from myself.

Ok, enough self exploration and analysis! This is what happened, and I can tell you, I felt a whole lot better for it!

So instead of feeling the usual stress, the need to answer her straight away, I felt calm and prepared! Because I had been on the course, and I knew what assertive behaviour was and how it went!

So when she asked me to have the boys this was what I said, 'Well, I'm not sure what I'm doing that day, give me ten minutes while I find my diary and I'll get right back to you'.

Ooh, do you see how clever that is?! Giving yourself a little space to consider the request, and decide whether you can, or can't, or whether you actually want to say yes is hugely important.

I put the phone down and sat and thought. I already knew that I was actually free that day for a while, but I had planned to do some things for myself, and I would have to rearrange some stuff, and cut my time short. I did love my nephews, but they were sometimes hard work. So I really thought deeply about whether I should have them that day and forgo my plans, or whether I actually needed that time for myself. I didn't get a lot of free time, and it was very precious to me. So, on this occasion I decided to say no.

And quite honestly, this was probably going to be the first time I was going to refuse her! I took a few moments and planned what I was going to say, and it felt much better being prepared than feeling on the spot and not knowing how to say no. So, I called back, and when she answered I took a deep breath and said 'I checked my plans for that day, and I'm so sorry not to be able to help this time, but I'm busy'.

Well, this obviously wasn't what she wanted to hear. And although I was trying to acknowledge that this might cause her a problem by apologising for not being able to help, she responded in the usual way, saying that she had no one else to ask, and if I didn't have them she didn't know what she would do.

Well, I didn't like hearing this, but also knew that I wasn't strictly true, and she did have other people she could ask. I just knew that I needed to assert myself, and so I repeated what I'd already said, adding that I could see it was difficult for her, but was really sorry I couldn't help this time.

She obviously wasn't all that happy, but we chatted for a while and then ended the conversation. I remember sitting there for a while kind of analysing my feelings. Did I feel guilty? Honestly yes I did, just a little. But I also knew that I had a right to my own time and I had a right to say no if I wanted to. I felt a bit worried that I had made her angry - but that was a risk I was prepared to take, and it wasn't as if I was being unreasonable or harsh or rude, I was just saying I couldn't help out on that particular day. All in all, I was pretty pleased with myself, as I felt I had handled it well. I had said no, and the sky hadn't fallen in. A big moment for me - risking someones disapproval, but it had all worked out pretty well so I knew I could do it again, and again.

Defining assertive, aggressive and passive behaviour

Assertive

Assertiveness is about standing up for your own, or other peoples rights in a calm and positive way. It's about expressing your feelings, wishes and desires effectively, without being aggressive, or just passively accepting what might not feel right. And it's being able to do this whilst being respectful and mindful of the thoughts, feelings and beliefs of others at the same time. Assertiveness can help you to express yourself in a clear, open and reasonable way, without giving your power away, nor taking on others issues. It is a powerful communication skill that enables you to act in your own best interests and to stand up for yourself without bad feeling or undue anxiety. You can also express honest feelings comfortably, and recognise your own personal rights without denying the rights of others.

Aggressive

Well, this kind of speaks for itself, but to sum it up, aggressive behaviour means a person is not particularly good at considering the views or feelings of other individuals, which can result in that persons rights and self esteem being undermined.

Aggressive behaviour is about getting what you want, no matter what. Communicating and acting in this way can include telling rather than asking, ignoring someone or speaking over them, pushing or rushing them for a decision or answer, and failing to consider their feelings. It will rarely demonstrate praise or appreciation of others, and tends to put the other person down. Aggressive responses can also encourage non assertive responses. as the person involved will be aggressive in return, or maybe just completely passive.

Passive

Passive responses are classically offered by those individuals who basically just say 'yes' when they actually want to say 'no'. Always complying with the wishes of others, wanting to please them can just undermine the individuals rights, and very importantly, their self confidence. Many people respond passively because they have a strong desire to be liked and approved of by others. They don't see themselves as 'equals' and they see other peoples rights, wishes and feelings as more important than their own. This then makes it hard to communicate their own thoughts and feelings, resulting in them doing things they don't really want to do in the hope that they might please someone. It can also mean that they allow others to take responsibility, lead them, and make decisions for them.

Of course, the underlying causes of passive behaviour are often low self confidence and self esteem - but over time, a downward spiral is created because is you don't present yourself positively, belittle or put yourself down in some way, you will inevitably feel inferior. Therefore your feelings of self worth are further reduced, so the spiral continues pulling you further down.

For example: Your partner says, 'Could you find time to wash the car today - it really needs a clean!

A typical passive response might be 'Yes, I'll do it after I've been shopping, called the doctor, made lunch for the kids and walked the dog...' Quite clearly, this person is feeling overwhelmed, busy, put upon, and doesn't really have the time at all - but they feel unable to state this fact and say no.

A more assertive response would be 'No, I can't do it today as I've already got a lot of things I need to do... yes, I agree, it's filthy! Maybe we could do it together at the weekend?'

This involves considering the request to wash the car in light of the list of other things they know they have to do, and then

valuing their own time - and themselves - enough to say no!

Mobile phones and the internet

I just want to mention an area with our children that can be very tricky to handle nowadays. Managing their use of internet access, gadgets and phones could require a lot of patience and a very assertive approach!

There are all kinds of guidelines about screen time and how the light affects our ability to sleep, isn't good for our eyes etc. And of course that is very relevant.

But there are other dangers and challenges as well.

When I think about my life as a child and a teenager and compare it today, I realise there is one thing that was really very different.

We didn't have mobile phones. Or Internet access. Or tablets. Or any kind of social media. We met our friends mostly at school, and if we were doing something with them outside of school they phoned us or came to call for us.

So if I had a bad day at school, was feeling upset, overwhelmed, or even bullied, at the end of the day I would go home to the sanctuary and safety of my house. And when I walked through my front door I'd go upstairs and shut out the world. I could hide in my bedroom and get away from it all.

The only way my friends could contact me would be by ringing the house on the landline. And if didn't want to talk to them I could always ask my mum to say I was out, or in the bath, or ill...

But nowadays we are attached to our phones as if they are some kind of umbilical cord. We take them with us everywhere and it is almost as if they have become a third limb that we just can't do without.

So my question is this.

If your child or teenager has had a bad day, where do they go to escape? Because even if they shut themselves in their bedroom, the phone is in there with them.

And that means the whole world is there with them too.

There really is no respite from the constant messages, Facebook, Instagram, Snapchat... Cyber bullying, cyber trolls, pressure from advertisements, it's all there and totally unavoidable unless they switch it all off. And how often do they do that? Honestly, when you think about it properly, it's pretty scary.

And it's a hard thing for kids to deal with.

There is the fear of not being good enough because they don't have as many friends as their peers on Facebook

How many people will like their post?

Will anyone say anything nice about their photos?

It all becomes a representation of their popularity, their value and their worth.

It's hard enough being a teenager, transitioning from child to adult and managing all the pressure and changes without having the world watching and commenting too!

And then thinking of the dangers of children and young people being targeted by older predators - quite simply, when your child has their phone in their room at night, you never know who is in the room with them.

And that is very worrying indeed.

So, my advice would be to create a family rule of keeping phones or tablets out of bedrooms, at least after a certain time.

Look, I know this won't be popular... but think carefully about it and decide what you as the parent want for their best interests.

Again, this goes back to being the one in charge, the responsible adult, the parent with the personal power and the ability to say no because it's best for your child. Be brave. Do what you know is right for them.

Your moment of Sunshine

Please don't worry if all of this doesn't make sense right away. Things often take a little practice, and you may want to reread this chapter another time. The beauty of it is purely and simply, you can't get it wrong. Every moment, every breath, every step, every day is a new start. An opportunity for change, learning, moving forward. So, just be good to yourself, and tell yourself how amazing you are. Remember, you are a human being, and a human doing your best. And that is good enough.

Your Golden Rule

Think about what you want and what you need, and don't be afraid to assert yourself. You are a valuable, wonderful person in this world with as much right as every single other person alive to feel happy and fulfilled. You deserve to feel good, you deserve to be loved. And don't forget that this starts with yourself. Go back to the mirror, look at yourself and say again 'I love and approve of myself and I deserve to be happy.' And start believing it!

CHAPTER
NINE

CO PARENTING AFTER
DIVORCE OR SEPARATION

Such a sad and difficult time for everyone involved. So much hurt, pain, sadness and grief. Which often is masked by anger and frustration all based on fear.

Your life has changed beyond all recognition. You are not longer part of a family, you are coping on your own at home, dealing with day to day difficulties without your partner. Life can be very tough.

You also may be feeling betrayed, let you down, cheated on, and in all honestly you never want to see or speak to them again.

But then there are the children. Those innocent little beings that rely on the both of you, love the both of you.

How can you put your feelings to one side and make things work as two separate parents instead of the unit you once were? How on earth do you carry on being civil with your ex?

Of course, if it weren't for the children you wouldn't have any reason to have to see each other or have contact, so it would be easier to get over what has happened. But because of them, you're still tied together. Not just financially, but there is still a massive emotional investment. Understandably, this can create feelings of anger, fear and disempowerment, and you can feel out of control of your life.

So how do you carry on? How to find a way to feel better? How do you come to terms with what has happened, but let it go? For the sake of the children?

Because at the end of the day this is what you're going to need to do.

If you carry on focusing on what has happened and your feelings about it, the children are going to suffer.

Sorry, but there's no way of sugar coating that.

Your children need you to put them first. And to do that, you are going to have to deal with what you are feeling as positively as you possibly can, and focus on making things more comfortable and easier for them

It may be that you both have very different attitudes to the children, their wellbeing, how to best care for them, and you feel that you aren't going to be able to 'change' each other. It didn't happen when you were together, how on earth can it happen now?

So this adds a greater burden to you as you end up arguing and tussling over who's way is best, who is letting them down, who is the better parent.

You're under pressure to be the best parent you can be every day whilst still trying to deal with the fall out from the emotional pressure you feel from it all.

As parents, our instinct is to protect our children from harm. We want to shield them from disappointment, upset and being let down.

So, now we really have to step up to the plate.

Although it may seem like an impossible ask, the very best thing for you, and your children, would be to work on letting all these terrible, negative feelings go. They will serve no purpose for you in the long run, only keep you stuck in the place you were trying to get away from in the first place. And of course, this isn't easy.

But part of your responsibility as a parent is to try your very best not to get in the way of their relationship with the other parent. Try to help them feel as comfortable and secure as possible with loving their two parents who aren't together any more. This isn't a competition. This isn't about proving who is the better parent, who got it right or wrong, who broke the relationship up, who do the children love the most.

This is now about damage limitation, and making the process of dealing and living with separated parents as easy as possible for your children.

There will probably be issues around access, parental responsibility, child support. But your children don't need to hear about this because it's nothing to do with them. What they need is for you to work it out between you and not involve them in the process.

If they hear you screaming and shouting and arguing, how will they end up feeling? If they hear you criticizing and abusing each other, how will they end up feeling?

Vocalising your frustrations and anger only it makes it harder for them. They may end up feeling guilty when they spend time with the other parent because they love you and want to be loyal to both, but feel they are 'betraying' one parent by being with the other.

And think about this. There will be times when your ex is pushing your buttons. They will say things that you feel are unfair, unjust, unnecessary, unkind. The battle of words and feelings will be hard to deal with, but when you allow yourself to respond with vicious, angry, hateful words then all that is happening is you are *giving away your personal power.*

This is the absolute truth. Once you have lost control, you have no power.

Now, I am not suggesting for a moment that you don't have the right to respond, the right to be upset, the right to stand your corner. Of course you do. We don't deserve to be attacked or put down or treated unfairly. But what I am saying is, it does you no good. Honestly, once you are screaming and shouting arguing back then you have engaged in the battle and there really is no winner. And certainly, it isn't the children.

Now, this may sound totally crazy, but I want you to know that you *have a choice* about how you decide to react, although it really may not feel like it. How are you supposed to stop yourself? It can feel out of your control as if you are going to explode with frustration and the injustice of what they might be saying to you, so you don't have a choice. But if you can stop yourself from responding negatively, stop yourself from saying the things they expect you to say, stop yourself from allowing the argument to go on and on and on, then you will coming from your place of personal power, and that is so important. You **do** have a choice, and it's up to you to make a good one.

So, your children will look to you to help them deal with their feelings about it all, and if you can help them to manage this they will love and respect you even more. Regardless of the things they might say to you when they are upset, this is the truth. They may well lash out at you at times, blame you, and be angry. But this is because they are hurt, sad, frightened, disappointed, and you are the person they can truly trust and show these feelings to.

Your heart will ache when you see their disappointed faces if the other parent lets them down. The pain of their sadness can be crushing. And you may feel so angry about your exes short comings and failings when it comes to being reliable, on time, capable and competent.

But you finding your strength, managing and dealing with these feelings without showing your children how you really feel is your most wonderful gift to them.

Aren't our children the most important, precious little beings? And don't they deserve to grow up feeling peaceful and positive with parents who will put them first?

Yes they do. And so that is why you can do this.

Positive, pleasant, powerful… that is going to be your mantra.

Repeat it to yourself daily, say it ten times a day! Make it happen. You can do it because you have your children's best interests at the forefront of *everything*, and you are a strong, loving parent and human being So, while you are giving your children that wonderful gift of doing what's right for them, make sure you do what's right for you too.

Look after *you*. Support *you*. You are such a massively, crucially important person in this world, and not just for your children, but as a person in your own right as well. You need to give yourself time and space to find support for yourself while you learn to cope with it all.

Talk to someone about it, get things off your chest, don't bottle it up and let it fester away inside you. See a counsellor if you feel you need to. There's no shame in talking to a caring, but impartial person. They can help you deal with how you're feeling and manage things better. Friends and family can also be a great support, although unlike a counsellor they may want to talk a lot and think they have all the answers for you! But the thing is, we are all unique and individual, and no one can know just how we feel. Others may have had a similar experience and dealt with it in their own way, but they really don't know exactly how you are feeling, no one does. It's up to you to work out how to more forward in the ways that works for you, to make your own choices and decisions, and to trust your own instincts.

Also, it's important at this time to look after yourself. Not just physically but emotionally as well. You will be going through a mourning process. You're probably still be grieving for the person that you thought and hoped your partner was, the disappointment of what has happened, what you feel you have lost.

Alternatively, you may be sitting there thinking 'what rubbish, I'm just furious, frustrated, and glad to be rid of her/him.' But these feelings cover up our pain, and it's ok to acknowledge that pain. When something ends, it's alright to feel sad. We aren't robots who can just turn our feelings off when we feel like it.

So let's go back to what we looked at earlier in the book about having faith, and I think it is worth repeating.

Be kind to yourself.

Focus your precious energy on creating positive changes in the now, this moment, and in the moment after that.

And you're going to take it one breath, one step, one day at a time.

Start the process off by giving yourself a great big loving pat on the back, just because you're you, and you deserve it. Take a few moments to sit and think about all the hard work you put in every single day. Remind yourself you are doing your best. Focus on what you have done well, and think about the positive achievements that you *do* make, all the time. I mean, come on, it's pretty amazing that you still make it through the day, you put food on the table, do the washing, go to work, or work at home, help someone with their homework, mow the lawn, call your mum, feed the cat, walk the dog, take the kids to ballet, wash the car. Remember, without a doubt, all of these are positive achievements, and it's you that is making it all happen. So you need to acknowledge this, and reward yourself.

Go to a yoga class, or zumba, or aqua fit, or take a walk in the sunshine. Play sport, get involved in games, have fun! Book yourself a reflexology session, a facial, a massage, a head rub, a pedicure or manicure. Watch a funny film, find something to laugh at, smile at people in the street. Make time to relax. Lie down, stretch, breathe deeply and slowly. Have a beautiful hot bath, light some candles, eat and drink something delicious. Because you are worth it, and you deserve it!

Have faith in yourself, and believe that things will get better, and little by little, they will. And how are you doing this? That's right - one breath, one step, one day at a time. Don't expect massive changes straight away. It might take a little time and practice to get this new attitude going, and you may well take a step forward, and then one back again. But remember what we said, this is just life, and it doesn't mean you're failing again or doing it all wrong. You're dancing your way through life - step forward, step back, shake your hips, cha cha cha!!

Your moment of Sunshine

And although your heart hurts to see their pain, your children will survive and they will be alright. Unfortunately, everyone has to learn to deal with disappointment, loss and sadness in life. We mourn, we grieve, we experience turmoil and fear, and this happens to children too. But all you can do is just carry on being there for them. Give them love, reassurance, and permission to express how they are feeling. And if you do this with calm, loving energy, encouragement and positive support, then it doesn't get much better than that. Every day is an opportunity for change. Every day we learn and grow. So what might seem like a never ending nightmare right now can and will come to an end. Hold on tight, have faith, and believe in yourself. These may well be difficult times, but if you can stay in your personal powerful place and work on making things the best they can be, then your children will know you were always there, always supporting them, always loving them.

Your Golden Rule

Find your personal power and stand strong so that you can make the best of a situation that you won't change with anger and negativity. Keep telling yourself how amazing you are, and believe it, because you are.

Keep looking for the sunshine, acceptance, forgiveness and love.

CHAPTER
TEN

FEELING PUT UPON?
THEN FIND YOUR
PERSONAL POWER!

'Am I Britain's most put-upon mother?'

'A howl of rage (and resentment) that'll strike a chord with countless exhausted women caught between elderly relatives, a lazy husband and children that won't fly the nest'

This was the introduction to the article entitled 'Am I Britain's most put-upon mother?' written by Liz Collins

Liz described how hard life was when everyone expected her to be there to do everything, be everything, drop everything and run after everyone else. She had an elderly relative who relied heavily on her, a husband with somewhat archaic views about mens and womens roles in the home, and two grown up children living at home.

Liz was tired. In fact, she sounded exhausted! And her point was that none of the people she loved seemed to notice this. She was there at their beck and call, feeling put upon and taken for granted.

Ok, so let's have a look at this whole situation.

How do we become 'put upon?' How do we end up running around after everyone else with no time for ourselves, no joy, no 'me time', feeling unappreciated and taken for granted?

How does this happen? Is it that the people around us are lazy, selfish, unkind, uncaring? Are we just unlucky and have to put up with it? Is just symptomatic of our generation, is just our lot in life and we have no say over it and no way of changing it?

Or - hold on a moment - radical thought here - is it us that actually creates the beast that we see before us?!

Because although this is only my humble opinion, I will share it with you. Surely we can only be put upon if we *ALLOW* ourselves to be put upon?

If all we ever do is run round after our loved one and sort out their lives by doing everything for them then we're not encouraging or empowering them to do things for themselves.

If we let them think that we are always available, always ready to ignore our own needs in favour of theirs, then we are telling them we are just a doormat and they can treat us as they please.

Quite simply, if they have someone running around cooking, clearing up after them, doing their washing, making appointments for them, bailing them out when they make a cock up, picking them up when they've had one too many to drive, then what would motivate them to do any of these things for themselves or take responsibility for their actions?

Now of course there's a balance between being kind and supportive and lovely and loving - but then just being a doormat. Sorry, that doesn't sound like a nice term, but I've been searching for something else that fits, and can't find it.

So, you put-upon women - would you like to make a change? Would you like to become Amazon, assertive, powerful women in charge of your destiny and making wonderful positive changes to your life?

Of course you do!

Pause for a moment… if you are the male of the species and have reached this far in the book then that's brilliant. I truly hope you are enjoying it and finding your personal power in all areas of life. Big up to you, good on you, and I'm delighted you're here. However, I would just like to ask you to excuse me for a few moments as I speak to my gals. Thank you for your patience and understanding. You're a top guy!

So my darlings, I wonder how many of you this will resonate with?

I can't help but think that many women seem to spend a lot their lives feeling guilty. For something, anything, everything! Possibly this is more true of women from my generation and before - but even so, many younger women I know seem to feel guilty about all sorts of things.

It almost feels as if we were weaned onto a diet of guilt, accompanied by some large doses of low self esteem, topped off with a nasty gooey dessert consisting of a belief that we are just not good enough!

And if I am offending anyone here I'm really sorry - but often this appears to be true.

We are only here for everyone else, and any time that we take for ourselves is 'selfish'.

We have to put everyone else first, to the detriment of our own well being, our own time and space, our own feelings.

We are the carers, the nurturers, the givers, and our needs must come last.

But hang on a minute - times have changed, attitudes have changed, women have changed, so we know it doesn't have to be like that.

So looking at this article, and this feeling of being 'put upon' that so many women seem to experience, what can we do?

How do we make changes to empower ourselves and feel less taken for granted?

Well, let's think about taking some steps towards making positive changes, whilst finding a way to say NO instead of YES all the time.

Again, not easily accomplished, again it might take some practice. But it is totally possible, and you can do this. Have a look back at the chapter about assertiveness, it's all in within your grasp!

I remember that someone once told me that we have to learn to say 'no' occasionally for the word 'yes' to mean something.

I wasn't sure what this meant at first. But when you think about it, maybe it makes sense? I guess if all we ever do is say yes to everyone and everything, but secretly we are feeling put upon and taken for granted, then we are really only saying yes with resentment and a negative feeling. So what good does that do us?

None at all, in my view!

And it provides the people around us with the impression that we *are* just doormats, there to do anything, anytime, and our only value is for our service to other people and not as an independent person in our own right.

Oh, don't get me wrong - of course we are loved. Our family love us, and would probably be shocked if they thought that we felt this way.

But somehow it seems as if there is a little fear inside us that that their love will be diminished, threatened, maybe even withdrawn if we say no to them.

Living with fear is soul destroying. It eats away at us, and taints everything we do.

Thinking back to my situation with my sister in law - oh yes, I was Queen Martyr! Poor me - being put upon, having to look after her children when I didn't want to, when I was tired, when I had my own stuff to deal with. But I didn't say no, I just carried on moaning about it and feeling negative. Until, of course, I learned about being assertive.

Now, saying no takes practice. It won't necessarily happen overnight. But just tackling one thing at a time means you can start making changes.

And as always, this will happen one breath, one step and one day at a time.

So, relating to article that Liz wrote - feeling guilty when you 'steal' a few hours to spend with a friend and are then constantly interrupted is no good for you. She described how taking any time for herself resulted in people constantly calling her, messaging, wanting something from her and she felt guilty for not just being at their beck and call.

So my advice to her would have been - turn your phone off! Or at least put it on silent if you are worried about emergencies. Concentrate on enjoying yourself and ignore endless messages. Don't be totally accessible to everyone all the time because that gives away your personal power, your personal value. And you're not stealing anything - you are enjoying some valuable time for the important person that is YOU!

If your mum rings when you're busy or doing something for yourself then let her know you can't speak right now. Tell her how lovely it is to hear from her. Tell her you will call her back later and have a good catch up. Yes, she lives alone, is getting older, her health isn't as good as it was. She may be feeling lonely and it's hard to think of her on her own. But *YOU* have a right to a life as well, and every day you're doing your best to love and support her. So if you are replenished by spending some time doing something for yourself, then you will feel better and she will also benefit from your positive, reinforced energy.

Why would you deny yourself a well earned glass of wine in the evening?!

Well, Liz's daughter would often go out for a drink with her mates, but then couldn't drive home as she was over the limit. But she always took the car because she knew her mum would come and collect her. So Liz would anticipate the late night call asking for a lift and would make herself available every time.

Liz… tell her to get a taxi! Or a lift with a friend! *YOU* aren't a taxi driver, you are a woman with her own life and the right to a glass of wine if you want one! And in time, your daughter will learn to make better plans and preparations for an evening out. It's all about the learning curve, and if you just rush off to pick her up and sort it all out for her every time, how will she ever learn?!

Liz's son needed to make an appointment with his gp. He was a student at uni - old enough and perfectly capable of calling and making it for himself. But Liz did it for him, and spent two hours on the phone trying to book it.

She would also spend a lot time trying to help him manage his assignment diary and keep it updated, and was frustrated by his seeming inability and disinterest.

Well Liz - quite simply, don't spend two hours on the phone trying to book his appointment - tell him to do it himself! And while you're at it, tell his to keep his assignment diary up to date! If you take responsibility for all these things, how will he ever learn to do it for himself? So he may not get his acne cream, or his assignment may be late.

Well this would only be the results of *his* choice, and he would soon learn to do it for himself if he had to accept and deal with the consequences of *his* actions!

And finally, what else could you do if your husband just sits and watches tv and reads the paper all day, and refuses to help out with what he deems as 'women's chores?'

Well, have a go at being assertive and asking for some assistance. But if this doesn't seem to float his boat, alternatively you could leave all his pants and socks out of the wash until he doesn't have any clean ones left, and then show him how to work the washing machine whilst laughing at the fact that he has to go commando until he's washed them!

Quite seriously, why should you do it all?

And the thing to remember is that none of the above has to be said or done with anger.

Keep it friendly, firm, encouraging and positive.

But stay true to yourself.

Find your personal power.

Just let the people you know and love that you actually value yourself enough to not be their doormat, and they will love and value you more.

Put-upon women? How about we start changing that to Amazon women, standing in our power, making positive change, loving ourselves and the world around us. Ladies - let's go!

And gentlemen - thank you for your loving support!

<u>Remember this:</u>

To '**Let Go**' doesn't mean to stop caring.... it just means I don't need to do it for someone else

To '**Let Go**' is not to care for.... but to care **about**

To '**Let Go**' is to learn, understand and **accept** that I can't and don't need to control another

To '**Let Go**' is not to try to fix.... just try to be there and be supportive

To '**Let Go**' is not to be in the middle arranging all the outcomes.... but to allow others to affect their own destinies

To '**Let Go**' is not to enable.... but to allow learning from natural consequences

To '**Let Go**' is not to try to change or blame another.... it is to accept and love without judgement.

To '**Let Go**' is not to be protective.... it is to permit another to face reality

To '**Let Go**' is not to deny, but to accept

To '**Let Go**' is to take each day as it comes and cherish myself in it

To '**Let Go**' is not to regret the past, or to focus on the future - but to be truly present in **THIS** moment, and then the next and the next....

To '**Let Go**' is to fear less.... and love more

To '**Let Go**' is to free myself from others expectations and blame

To 'Let Go' is to accept myself and love myself exactly as I am

Today is the first day of the rest of your life - please
make it a good one because you deserve it.

Here's to you finding your positive, personal power.

Here's to creating greater balance
and harmony in your life.

Here's to your happiness, joy, and laughter.

And here's to warm, replenishing Sunshine 4 your Soul.

I truly hope that this book has provided you with what
you wished for, some guidance and support to make some
positive changes, whilst learning how to love and appreciate
yourself! And I hope that your soul is now filled with
Sunshine.

Please let me know how you get on, I will be waiting to
hear from you!

May your life be filled with sunshine, blessings and
everything you deserve.

Marion Ingerson-Heart xxx

ABOUT THE AUTHOR

Marion believes that everyone deserves Sunshine 4 their Soul. Her unique book is based son her life experiences and the lessons she's learned and benefited from. With equal measures of frankness, honesty and self deprecating humour, Marion invites to you read about her childhood, her family, her rebellious teenage years, her parenting years... and offers you the opportunity to explore yours whilst giving you the tools to make positive changes.

With over 25 years experience of working with teenagers, Marion passionately believes that the behaviours they display are just their way of acting out their hidden emotions and fears and asking for help and guidance. Investing time, energy and love in our young people today means that tomorrow the world can be better, for them, for you, and for us all. Marion believes that is our responsibility as parents to set the clear, healthy, positive boundaries and rules that our children need. And if we replace negativity and hopelessness with a positive outlook and faith in the outcome, we will succeed in changing family relationships for the better.

But the place to start is with yourself. Finding self belief, self acceptance, self love...

Marion didn't have these - but she was superwoman. She flew around assisting, helping, sorting, advising her family and friends - whether they wanted her to or not! With painful honesty Marion recalls moments from her life that she would possibly rather forget. But what she has tried to take from every experience is the lesson to be learned and how to move forward. And how to work on loving herself.

No longer superwoman. Just a caring, passionate, insightful woman. Willing and happy to share her story and advice with you in the hope that you may find a little personal Sunshine 4 your Soul - just one breath, one step, and one day at a time.